Come
and
Dine

Bluff Dale Baptist Church
150 Years of Amazing Cooks

Compiled by Wanda Strange

Cover photo by Cheryl Barron

Clip art used in this book were purchased from Bigstock.com or compliments of Pix-abay.com.
Thank you, artists, for generously sharing your talents.

Cover and interior design by Radical Women

Many of the members of Bluff Dale Baptist Church were also members of the Bluff Dale Study and Garden Club. These ladies and their friends and neighbors supported community events like the Annual Ice Cream Social and Annual Community Thanksgiving Dinner. In 1999 and 2010, The Bluff Dale Study and Garden Club compiled cookbooks to which its members contributed. Some of the recipes in the "Come and Dine" compilation were originally submitted to "Paluxy Valley Cookbook" or "Meals and Memories." These recipe compilations include delicious dishes and can be obtained from the garden and study club.

Published by Radical Women

Radical Women
PO Box 782
Granbury, TX 76048
www.bylisabell.com
email: LisaBell@bylisabell.com

Print ISBN: 979-8988648574
eBook ISBN: 979-8988648581

As Bluff Dale Baptist Church celebrates 150 years, we remember those who came before.

This collection of stories and recipes honors the memory of generations who left a legacy of faith in the Bluff Dale Community. Our generation stands on their shoulders, desiring that we be found faithful to continue that legacy and pass it on to the next generation.

Jesus saith unto them, Come and dine. (John 21:12 KJV.)

Contents

Introduction

Recipe for Preserving Children

Submitted by LaNell McNaughten

1 large grassy field
6 children
3 small dogs
Flowers
Narrow strip of brook with pebbles
Hot sun
Deep blue sky

Mix the children with the dogs and empty fields, stirring continuously.

Sprinkle the field with flowers, pour the brook gently over the pebbles.

Cover all with a deep blue sky and bake in hot sun. When children are well browned, they may be removed.

Will be found right for setting away to cool in bathtub.

The term "potluck" originated in the 15th century. The original meaning was quite literal. Travelers or guests who arrived unannounced relied on "the luck of the pot." They ate whatever the family served or in some cases left in the pot on the stove, or they went hungry.

The practice of group meals where guests bring food contributions has existed as long as societies have gathered for community events such as weddings, funerals or other common gatherings. The common tradition we continue to enjoy became popular in the late 18th century. In some regions, these events are called covered dish suppers, Jacob's suppers, or Jacob joins. Though no definitive evidence identifies an origin of the Jacob connection, some sources suggest it has to do with the Biblical story of Jacob tricking his brother, Esau, out of his birthright with an offering of food.

Though no documentation exists of anyone losing a birthright at the BDBC potlucks, the times and food we share around the tables serve to bond us together as a church family.[1]

---

1. [1] (Bramen, 2010)

Sweet and Savory Snacks and Appetizers

Peach Sweet Pickles

From the Kitchen of Laura Dameron

This recipe for Peach Sweet Pickles came from the 1936 cookbook, "How We Cook West of the Pecos."

Select large clingstone peaches. Pare about 10 lbs of peaches, add 3 lbs sugar, 1 qt vinegar, 2 oz stick cinnamon. 1 oz each of cloves and allspice (stick cloves in each peach). Boil until tender, remove and drain fruit. Cook syrup and thicken. Drop peaches back into hot syrup and seal at once.

Crab Toast

Submitted by Nelda Estes to "Meals and Memories"

Nelda attributes this recipe to her sister-in-law, Val Evans. This appetizer wins rave reviews at every potluck, family reunion, and ladies luncheon. No one can crab about this one. Enjoy!

1 stick butter, room temperature
1 can crab meat
1 jar Old English cheese (Kraft)
1 ½ Tbsp Mayonnaise
½ tsp garlic powder
¼ tsp celery seed
½ tsp pepper
1 Tbsp minced onion
4 English Muffins

Mix well. Spread on split English Muffins. Bake at 350 degrees for 20 minutes or until bubbly. Cut into fourths.

Crisp Pecan Crackers

Submitted by E & R Fudge & Co

½ cup cold butter
2½ cups flour
2 large eggs
1 tsp Tabasco Sauce
1 tsp Worcestershire Sauce
2 Tbsp minced green onion
1 cup grated sharp cheddar cheese
½ cup grated Parmesan cheese
½ cup chopped pecans

Cut cold butter into flour using a food processor or manually by using a knife and fork until mixture is well blended. In a small bowl, beat eggs, tabasco sauce and Worcestershire sauce together. Add egg mixture, onion, cheeses and pecans to flour/butter mixture.

When all ingredients are blended, form dough into a log. Wrap dough in plastic wrap and freeze for an hour.

Preheat oven to 350 degrees.

Slice pecan log into very thin rounds and place onto lightly greased baking sheet. Bake until lightly browned.

Yield: about 30 crackers

Sausage Balls

Submitted by LaNell McNaughten

2 lb sausage
3 Cups Bisquick
10 oz grated cheddar cheese

Mix well. Roll into balls. Bake on cookie sheet at 350 degrees until brown about 30 minutes. Makes 65 balls.

Hot Cheese Dip

Submitted by Terri Robinett

1lb Cheddar cheese, grated
1 medium onion, *finely* chopped
6 jalapeno peppers, cut fine and remove any seeds or stems (I use jalapeno slices from a jar)
Mayonnaise, enough to make it spread or dip (don't use salad dressing)
Dash of salt
Dash of pepper
Dash of sugar
Strawberry Preserves - chilled until ready to serve
Your favorite crackers for dips (Ritz or Triscuits are good!)

Keep the Strawberry Preserves cold until ready to serve. Combine all other ingredients and chill. To serve, take a cracker (Ritz or your favorite) and spoon some of the cheese spread on it. Then spoon a little bit of the strawberry preserves on top of it. It's delightful and addicting.

Puppy Chow

Submitted by Cheryl McCormick Rhoades

9 cups combination of corn, rice and wheat Chex cereal squares
1 cup chocolate chips
½ cup creamy peanut butter
¼ cup butter
2 tsp vanilla
1 ½ cups powdered sugar
2 one-gallon Ziplock bags

Place cereal in a large bowl and set aside. In a medium microwavable bowl, add chocolate chips, peanut butter and butter. Microwave on high for 1 minute and stir. Microwave 30 seconds longer and stir mixture until smooth. Stir in vanilla. Pour over cereal and stir until evenly coated. Spoon half the mixture in each one-gallon bag. Add ¾ cup powdered sugar to each bag and seal. Shake the bag until everything is coated. Spread on waxed/parchment paper to cool. Store in airtight container.

Lemonade Puppy Chow

Submitted by LaNell McNaughten

Ingredients:
6 cups rice Chex cereal
1 cup white chocolate chips
¼ cup butter
Zest of 1 lemon
2 Tablespoons lemonade mix powder
½ cup powdered sugar (for coating)

Directions:
Place rice Chex cereal in large mixing bowl and set aside. In microwave-safe bowl, combine white chocolate chips and butter. Microwave in 30 second intervals, stirring between each interval, until melted and smooth.

Stir lemon zest and lemonade mix powder into the melted white chocolate mixture, pour over the rice Chex cereal, and gently stir until all the cereal is evenly coated. Place ½ cup powdered sugar in bag and shake until cereal is coated with powdered sugar.

Alex's Disappearing Mexican Shrimp Cocktail

Submitted by Melissa Saucedo

64 oz Clamato Juice

18 oz Ketchup

36 oz Orange Juice

(The best orange juice to use for this recipe is a bottle of the non-refrigerated orange juice, by the grape juice products at the store on the shelf, but feel free to use any orange juice. You will use anywhere from 1/2 to 3/4 of a 48 oz bottle)

Blend these liquids together, either in a blender a little at a time and mix or use an immersion blender. Adjust measurements to taste. You may need to add a little more orange juice or ketchup, a little at a time.

Finely Dice, Chop and Mix into juice mixture:

3 Tomatoes

1 Onion

Cilantro (tear off a handful of the cilantro leaves and roughly chop)

Mix in: (Previously Thawed & Drained)

1 lb of frozen peeled, deveined, tail-off medium cooked shrimp (thawed)

1 lb of frozen peeled, deveined, tail-off extra small cooked shrimp (thawed)

Tip: I thaw by placing a colander in the sink and letting cool water flow over the shrimp.

Optional Toppings:

2 Jalapenos

2 Avocadoes

Hot sauce; such as Cholula or Tapatio

Lime juice from a lime wedge

Saltines

-Alex Saucedo;
"Whatever you do, work at it with all your heart, as working for the Lord, not for human masters." (Colossians 3:23 NIV).

David's Quick Shrimp Ceviche

Submitted by Melissa Saucedo

Mix:

1-2 lbs of frozen, deveined, cooked extra small shrimp (thawed, or you can get medium and dice once thawed).
Juice of 2 limes
1 red onion (finely diced)
4 TBSP cilantro (finely chopped)
2 jalapenos (depending on heat, seed and devein)
2 avocados (diced)
2 TBSP of extra virgin olive oil
Optional: splash of orange juice or a dash of creole seasoning to make it your own.

Put ceviche on top of a tostada, eat with saltines or dig in with tortilla chips.

Top with hot sauce such as Valentina, Cholula or Tapatio and an extra squeeze of lime juice.

David Saucedo

"Do not conform to the pattern of this world but be transformed by the renewing of your mind. Then you will be able to test and approve what God's will is—his good, pleasing and perfect will.:" (Romans 12:2 NIV)

Special Gift of Love

When my mother died, Cynthia Brown asked me for one of Honey's garments. I gave her one of my mother's favorite denim dresses. A few weeks later, she showed up at my house. She had trimmed the dress all up and created the coolest apron I still use today.

Sherry Jacks

Salads

Tropical Chicken Salad

Submitted by E & R Fudge & Co

1 Can Chicken Breast 12.5 oz drained
1 Can Pineapple Chunks 8 oz drained
1 Can Mandarin Oranges 11 oz drained
1 stalk celery chopped
½ tsp. garlic powder
Pepper to taste
¼ cup pecans
1/3 cup mayonnaise
Break up chicken with a fork. Combine with pineapple, celery, garlic powder, pepper, pecans and mayonnaise. Stir until well mixed. Fold in mandarin oranges last or place on top. Serve on a lettuce leaf, sour dough bread or croissants.

Mexican Salad

Submitted by Georgia Scott
Originally submitted to the Paluxy Valley Cookbook

1 lb cooked ground beef
1 head lettuce
1 lb rat cheese (grated)
1 15-ounce ranch style bean (drained and chilled)
2 tomatoes (diced)
½ onion (chopped)
¾ bottle Kraft Catalina Dressing
1 small bag Fritos (crushed)
   Mix all except Fritos and chill well. Mix Fritos into chilled salad; serve immediately.

Strawberry Spinach Chicken Salad

Submitted by Renee Schott

2 Tbsp fresh lemon juice
½ tsp Dijon Mustard
½ cup extra virgin olive oil
Kosher salt to taste
Freshly ground black pepper to taste
2 cooked rotisserie chicken breasts (chopped into ½ inch pieces)
¼ small red onion thinly sliced
5 cups (about 5 ounces) packed baby spinach
2 cups thinly sliced strawberries
¾ cups of chopped, toasted pecans, divided
5 oz. feta, crumbled

In a large bowl, whisk lemon juice and mustard until combined. While whisking, slowly add oil until smooth and emulsified. Add salt and pepper.

Add chicken, onion, spinach, strawberries, and ½ cup of pecans. Toss to combine.

Divide salad onto plates. Top with remaining ¼ cup pecans and feta.

"Diversity is like a potluck dinner – everyone brings something different to the table, and together, we feast."
Kayla Woods, Pinson, Alabama

Broccoli Slaw

Submitted by Beverly Holmes

Lightly mix the following in a bowl:
    1 pkg. Broccoli slaw, 9 oz.
    1 medium apple, cored, peeled & chopped
    ½ cup pecans, toasted & chopped
    For dressing whisk together:
    1 cup mayonnaise
    2 Tbsp Apple Cider Vinegar
    ¼ cup of sugar
    Pour dressing over slaw and chill until serving.
    I have also used a commercially prepared coleslaw dressing with good results.

Babe's Salad

Submitted by Judy Bush

2 Tbsp sugar
1 tsp salt
¼ cup apple cider vinegar
2 Tbsp extra light olive oil
1 head iceberg lettuce
    Chill salad bowls.
    Mix all dressing ingredients in a jar. Chill dressing while chopping lettuce.
    Cut bite sized lettuce pieces. Put in chilled bowl.
    Pour in dressing and mix.
    Grind black pepper over the top.

Five Bean Salad

Submitted by E & R Fudge & Co

1 16 ounce can cut green beans, drained and rinsed
1 16 ounce can cut wax beans, drained and rinsed
1 15 ounce can kidney beans, drained and rinsed
1 15 ounce can garbanzo beans, drained and rinsed
1 16 ounce can baby limas, drained and rinsed
1 2-ounce jar pimentos, drained
1 cup chopped green pepper
1 cup chopped red onion
1 cup chopped celery
1 tsp minced garlic (or more to taste)
¾ cup apple cider vinegar
¼ cup sugar or Splenda
1 Tbsp vegetable oil
½ tsp salt
½ tsp freshly ground black pepper

Combine first 10 ingredients in a large bowl and toss well.

Combine vinegar, sugar, oil, salt and pepper in a small saucepan. Bring to a boil stirring constantly. Pour vinegar mixture over the bean mixture. Toss gently. Cover and chill at least 3 hours stirring occasionally. Will keep at least a week in the refrigerator.

When I was a young mother, not yet working outside my home, my church had a Baptist young women's group that met monthly. Many times, we ended with a salad luncheon. Our group advisor was also my Sunday School teacher and a retired school teacher. She always brought this salad, and I still make it on special occasions.
Bonnie Rucker

Lois' Five Way Salad

From the kitchen of Bonnie Rucker
As submitted to "Meals and Memories"

1 large can pineapple chunks, drained
1 large can mandarin oranges, drained
1 cup coconut
2 cups miniature marshmallows
1 small carton sour cream
  Mix well in a large salad bowl. Cover and chill for several hours before serving. Tastes just like ambrosia.

Corn Salad

Submitted by Glenda Sargent

3 cans Del Monte Sweet Corn (29 Oz. drained)
1 large sweet onion chopped fine
1 green or red bell pepper chopped fine
Salt (to taste)
Pepper (cracked pepper)
Hellman's Mayo (about 3 lg TBS)
1 bag Mexican four cheese blend finely grated
1 bag chili cheese Fritos 9.25 oz (Crushed)
  Mix the first three ingredients together, adding salt & pepper to taste. Add Mexican four cheese blend, then mayo. Stir well. (You will need enough mayo for the chili cheese Fritos to add right before serving.)
  It's awesome the next day! Enjoy!

Spinach Salad

Submitted by Cheryl McCormick Rhoades

1 cup slivered almonds
½ package fresh spinach
2 medium ribs of celery sliced thin
2 Tbsp and 2 tsp sugar
½ Head Romaine lettuce
2 green onions sliced thin
1 1 oz. can mandarin oranges (drained)

Cook almonds and sugar in heavy skillet until almonds are golden brown. Immediately spread onto a plate and separate. Tear lettuce and spinach together into a bowl; add almonds, oranges, green onion and celery.

Dressing for Salad

½ cup oil (olive or vegetable)
4 Tbsp White Vinegar
½ tsp salt
1 tsp parsley (dry or fresh, optional)
4 Tbsp Sugar
Dash pepper
Dash tabasco

Put all ingredients in jar and shake.
Do not refrigerate; serve at room temperature.
Pour over salad mixture just before serving.

"A recipe has no soul. You, as the cook, must bring soul to the recipe."

Thomas Keller

German Potato Salad

Submitted by Cynthia Brown

6 large potatoes (diced and cooked)
1 large onion
6 stalks of celery
1 lb bacon
1 cup vinegar
2 Tbsp flour
Salt and pepper to taste
   Fry bacon to crumble. Using bacon grease, sauté onion and celery.
   Heat flour and vinegar to thicken; pour over potatoes, add bacon.
Toss.
   Cover the top with Eckrich sausage. Cook until sausage is hot.

Coconut Ranch Kale Salad

Submitted by Renee Schott

¼ cup coconut milk
¼ vegan mayonnaise
1 Tbsp chopped parsley
1 Tbsp sliced chives
2 Tbsp chopped fresh dill
½ tsp garlic powder
¼ tsp onion powder
Pinch of cayenne pepper
Kosher salt
Freshly ground black pepper
1 large sweet potato – cut into ¼ inch half-moons
1 Tbsp, plus 2 tsp extra virgin olive oil, divided
1½ tsp chili powder, divided

1 can chickpeas, drained and rinsed

1 large bunch curly kale, stems removed and coarsely chopped

1 thinly sliced avocado and shaved vegan parmesan for serving

In small bowl whisk together milk, mayonnaise, parsley, chives, dill, garlic powder, onion powder, cayenne pepper, salt and black pepper. Refrigerate until ready to use.

Preheat oven to 400 degrees. On a large baking sheet, drizzle potatoes with 1 Tbsp oil, salt, ground black pepper, and 1 tsp chili powder. Toss to coat. Roast potatoes until tender and bottoms start to crisp. (about 35-40 minutes)

Meanwhile, pat chickpeas dry with paper towels and spread on a small baking sheet. Roast until crisp (about 30 minutes). While chickpeas are still warm, transfer to a medium bowl. Add 2 Tbsp oil and ½ tsp chili powder. Toss to combine. Season with salt and pepper.

In a large bowl, massage kale and a large pinch of salt with clean fingers until kale softens (about one minute). Top kale with potatoes, chickpeas, avocado, and parmesan. Drizzle with coconut ranch.

Lime Jello Salad

Submitted by Wanda Strange

My mother made this salad especially at holidays.

   1 container whipped topping (Cool Whip)

   1 container small curd cottage cheese

   1 package lime Jello

   1 large can pineapple chunks, drained

   1-2 cups nuts, your choice of pecans or walnuts. (optional)

Mix all the ingredients together and chill several hours prior to serving. It's particularly good the next day.

Southern Tater Salad

Submitted by Kerry Strange

5 lbs Russett Potatoes (about 8 medium potatoes)
1½ cup Miracle Whip
¼-½ cup mustard to taste
1 medium onion (chopped)
1 tsp salt (or more to taste)
1 small jar sweet pickle relish
4 hard-boiled eggs roughly chopped
4 slices bacon (fried and crumbled)
Paprika (optional, as desired)

Cut potatoes in halves or thirds and boil until fork tender. Drain. Mash potatoes (I use an electric mixer to blend well.) In a large bowl, fold potatoes together with Miracle Whip, mustard, onion, salt, pepper and other seasonings as desired. Fold in the pickles, eggs, and bacon.

Mandarin Orange Salad

Submitted by Cynthia Brown

2 cans pineapple chunks, drained
2 cans Mandarin oranges, drained
1 can angel flake coconut
1 cup sour cream
1 pkg miniature marshmallows

Mix fruit and coconut. Add sour cream. Add marshmallows last. Keep in refrigerator 24 hours before serving for best flavor.

Cornbread Salad

From the kitchen of Marionelle Frizzell
Submitted to "Meals and Memories"

I believe the secret to this recipe is the "corn-kits" and Hellmann's mayonnaise.
   1 package Morrison's Corn-Kits mix
   ½ cup chopped onion
   2 medium or one large bell pepper, chopped
   1 small can whole kernel corn
   3 slices bacon, cooked crisp and crumbled
   Hellmann's mayonnaise
   Prepare cornbread as directed on the package. Cook and crumble into large bowl and add the remaining ingredients. Add enough mayonnaise to moisten until the salad reaches a sticky consistency.

Coke Salad

Katie Sue Parker Recipe
Submitted by Rene Gresham

1 Can Bing Cherries, drain and reserve the juice
1 Can crushed Pineapple, drain and reserve the juice
2 packages cherry Jello
1 Can Coke
Pecans if desired
   Bring to a boil the juice of the cherries and pineapple. Pour over the Jello and stir until blended. Add other ingredients. Chill until set.
   Hint: use 12-ounce coke can. If pouring from a large bottle of coke, the total amount of liquid should not exceed 4 cups.
   This is a Gresham family favorite.

Grape Salad

Submitted by Sherry Jacks

1½ lb. Red Grapes
8 oz. cream cheese
8 oz. sour cream
1 Cup brown sugar
1/3 Cup sugar
1 cup chopped pecans or walnuts
2 Tbs. vanilla (yes TABLESPOON)
  Cream the cheese and sour cream. Add brown sugar and vanilla. Fold in grapes. Put in a serving dish and top with a mixture of sugar and nuts. Refrigerate.

  Note: I like to make it at least a day ahead and I use low-fat cream cheese and low-fat sour cream. It keeps for several days in the refrigerator, and I have frozen it for about 3 months before moving it to the refrigerator to defrost.

Melissa's Mamaw's Watergate Salad

Submitted by Melissa Saucedo

1 3.4oz pkg of instant pistachio pudding mix.
1 15-oz can crushed pineapple with juice.
1 8oz carton of Cool Whip.
1/2 C of chopped pecans.
Optional: shredded coconut or mini marshmallows.
  Mix all together and refrigerate until ready to eat.

  "At that time the son born according to the flesh persecuted the son born by the power of the Spirit. It is the same now." (Galatians 4:29 NIV)

"Gussy" Congealed Salad

Story and recipe submitted by Carol Richey

My mother, Eileen Rhoades, got this recipe from a relative named "Gussy." She made it for Christmas, and I continue the tradition. In many ways it is more dessert than salad. So, call it what you want and eat it when you want.

1 small package lemon Jello
1 cup cream, whipped
1 cup pecans, chopped
1 small can crushed pineapple
1 cup small curd cottage cheese

Make Jello as package directs but only chill until it is the thickness of egg whites.

Fold in other ingredients in Jello and refrigerate until solid.

At Christmas, I add green food coloring, pour into a wreath shaped mold, and decorate with maraschino cherries.

Chickpea Salad

Submitted Lisa Bell

1 can garbanzo beans (chickpeas)
1 small Roma tomato, chopped
Green onions (substitute part of a small onion), diced
Mini bell peppers, diced
1 TBSP mayonnaise or Miracle Whip
1 tsp mustard
Optional: other vegetables as desired

Mix all ingredients until evenly coated. Serve on a bed of fresh mixed greens.

Cranberry/Pineapple Salad

Submitted by Wanda Strange

This is a Strange family favorite. I make it for Thanksgiving. It's the only way my family will eat cranberry sauce.

1 can whole berry cranberry sauce
1 large can crushed pineapple
1 can sweetened condensed milk (Eagle brand)
1 container whipped topping (Cool Whip)
1-2 cups chopped nuts, pecans or walnuts (optional)

Mix all ingredients together until well blended. Spread into a 9x13" dish (I use a disposable dish for easy holiday cleanup) Freeze until solid. Cut into squares. (You can serve it unfrozen as a fruit side-dish. My family likes it best frozen. It will keep in the freezer for several weeks.)

Hot Pineapple Salad

Submitted by Elayne Jackson Block
As Submitted to Paluxy Valley Cookbook

1 20-oz can crushed pineapple, drained
3-4 TBSP flour
1/4-1/2 cup sugar
2 cups crushed Ritz crackers
1 stick butter
1-2 cups grated cheese

Mix pineapple, flour, and sugar together in baking dish. Combine crackers, butter, and cheese together and pour over pineapple mixture. Bake at 350 degrees for 20-30 minutes.

Fruit Salad for a Group

Submitted by Terri Robinett

(I got this from one of my TCU friends!)
1 can peach pie filling
½ pint frozen strawberries, undrained
1 bag frozen whole strawberries (or fresh strawberries)
1 bag frozen peaches (or fresh sliced peaches)
1 large can of pineapple chunks with juice
2 cups red grapes
2 cups green grapes
2-3 kiwi fruit (sliced)
About 6 large bananas sliced

Combine all ingredients (except bananas) in the order listed above. Chill. Add bananas before serving.

Soups

Cowboy Stew

Submitted by Scott and Cindi Pace

 *This was the meal served to us when we moved from seminary in Fort Worth to our first church in Jena, LA. Along with the Jena Banana Pudding (included in the dessert section) has been a family favorite ever since.*

Cindi Pace

Brown 1½ lbs ground beef
Add: 2 cans whole tomatoes
1 cup chopped onions
½ green pepper chopped
1 clove garlic crushed
1 tsp. salt
¼ tsp pepper
1 Tbsp chili powder
Simmer 20 minutes.
Add: 1 can whole kernel corn
1 can red kidney beans
2 cups cubed potatoes
Simmer another 20 minutes or until potatoes are done.

*"Here I am! I stand at the door and knock. If anyone hears my voice and opens the door, I will come in and eat with that person, and they with me." (*Revelations 3:20 NIV).

French Market Soup

Submitted by E & R Fudge & Co

MIX: ¼ cup each of the following dried beans
Black Beans, Baby Lima Beans, Pinto Beans
Kidney Beans, Split Peas, Navy Beans
Garbanzo Beans, Black-eyed Peas, Lentils
   Wash and drain. Place in a large bowl. Cover with water and 1 tsp salt.
   Soak overnight. Drain. Place in large soup pot.
Add:
3 quarts water
1 ham hock
2-3 bay leaves
½ tsp Thyme
   Cover. Bring to a boil. Let simmer for 3 hours
Add:
1 quart of canned tomatoes
2 medium onions, chopped
2 cloves of garlic minced
6 ribs celery chopped or sliced
Cayenne pepper and salt to taste
   Simmer uncovered for 1½ hours
Add:
1 lb smoked sausage
½ fryer
   Simmer until chicken is done. Remove chicken and sausage and cut into small pieces. Return to soup. Taste and adjust seasonings. 10 minutes before serving add 2 Tbsp parsley.

Easy Mulligan Stew

Submitted by Terri Robinett

2 lbs Ground Beef
1 Med Onion, Chopped
1 Can Tomatoes, chopped or squished with your fingers
2 Beef Bouillon Cubes
1 Can Green Beans
1 Can Peas
1 Can Corn
Couple shakes of Worcestershire Sauce
Salt and Pepper to taste

Brown ground beef with onion and drain fat. Add canned vegetables (do not drain vegetables). Add bouillon cubes and seasonings to taste. If soup is too thick add water. Simmer for about 20 to 30 minutes or while you make corn bread to go with!

Three Bean Spinach Soup

Submitted by E & R Fudge & Co

1 medium onion chopped
1 Tbsp vegetable oil
3 small potatoes, peeled and cubed
3 medium carrots, sliced
3 cans (14½ ounces each) chicken broth
3 cups water
2 Tbsp parsley flakes
2 tsp dried basil
1 tsp dried oregano
1 garlic glove, minced
½ tsp black pepper

1 can (15 oz) pinto beans, rinsed and drained
1 can (15½ oz) great northern beans, rinsed and drained
1 can (15 oz) garbanzo beans, rinsed and drained
3 cups chopped fresh spinach

In Dutch oven, sauté onion in oil. Add the next 9 ingredients. Simmer, uncovered, until vegetables are tender. Add beans and spinach; heat through.

Yield: 12 servings (about 3 quarts)

Tomato Basil Soup

Submitted by E & R Fudge & Co

4 cups canned whole or diced tomatoes or 8-10 medium fresh tomatoes peeled and boiled.
4 cups tomato juice or chicken stock. (I use half juice and half chicken stock) Stock can be fresh broth, canned chicken broth, or diluted chicken bouillon. (Broth is better than bouillon)
12-14 fresh torn basil leaves
1 stick butter
1 cup cream
Salt
Cracked black pepper

Bring tomato mixture to a boil. Reduce heat and simmer for 30 minutes.

Add basil to tomato mixture and puree in small batches in a blender or puree with hand blender in the pan.

Add butter and cream. Stir until butter is melted. Add salt and pepper to taste.

"Eating is a necessity, but cooking is an art."
Unknown

Chicken Tortilla Soup

Submitted by Cheryl McCormick Rhoades

Ingredients:

2-3 cups of raw chicken, cut into 1-inch pieces
1 can diced tomatoes with green chilies
1 (8 ounce) can tomato sauce
2 (14.5 ounce) cans chicken broth
1 can cheddar cheese soup
2 cups carrots (We used the "carrot chips" that are cut like pickles, and cut them in half)
½ bag frozen corn
1 large onion chopped
2 cloves garlic minced
½ tsp ground cumin
½ tablespoon chili powder
Cilantro (we just chopped up a handful)
Salt and pepper to taste

Garnishes:

2 avocados cut into small bites
Shredded cheese
Tortilla chips

Directions:

Combine all ingredients in the slow cooker, except for the garnishes. Cook on HIGH for about 5-6 hours or on LOW for about 8 hours. Ladle into bowls and top each serving with avocado, cheese, and tortilla chips.

Chicken Soup

Submitted by Cynthia Brown

I got this Chicken Soup Recipe about 40 years ago on a ski trip with friends. I have since revised it to suit my family and friends. My children say "It makes you well." It is the supreme comfort food.

Cynthia Brown

1 chicken – I cook in a crock pot. Cover chicken with water and cook on low 3-6 hours.

Using 4 cups chicken broth cook 2 cups celery and 2 large onions chopped (save the rest of the broth)

When celery is tender (about 20 minutes) add 1½ cups of dry rice

Add 2/3 cup chopped bell pepper. Cook until tender

Add and Heat:

1 large jar pimentos

2 16 oz cartons sour cream

1 quart whipping cream

Cooked chicken.

Salt and pepper to taste.

More broth may be added if you think soup is too thick.

"As for real chicken soup, I have it once or twice a week."

Jack Canfield

Chicken Poblano soup

Submitted by LaNell McNaughten

3 poblano peppers
¼ c butter
¼ c flour
2 (32 oz) cans chicken broth
2 c diced roasted chicken breasts
1 can corn
1 can black beans
1 can Rotel
2 c shredded sharp cheddar cheese
2 tsp garlic powder
Salt and pepper to taste
1 c sour cream
2 c tortilla chips for topping

Preheat oven's broiler and set the oven rack at about 6 inches from the heat source. Line a baking sheet with aluminum foil. Cut the peppers in half from top to bottom: remove seeds, stem and ribs, then place the peppers cut side down onto the prepared baking sheet. Cook under the broiler until the skin of the peppers has blackened and blistered. About 5 minutes. Place the blackened peppers into a bowl and tightly seal with plastic wrap. Allow the peppers to steam as they cool. About 20 minutes. Once cool, remove the skins and discard. Dice the roasted peppers.

While the peppers are cooling, melt the butter in a pot over medium heat. Whisk in flour and stir until the mixture becomes paste-like and light golden brown, about 5 minutes. Gradually whisk the chicken broth into the flour mixture and bring to a simmer over medium heat. Cook and stir until the mixture is thick and smooth. About 10 minutes.

Stir in the rest of the ingredients. Bring to a simmer and simmer until the cheese has melted and the soup is hot, about 10 minutes. Serve sprinkled with tortilla chips.

Creamy Potato Soup

From the kitchen of Hettie Jackson
As submitted to "Meals and Memories"

This original recipe is from Opal Harris Pittman, dear aunt to Hettie Harris Jackson, Anna Harris Watson, and Marionell Frizzell, all of Bluff Dale.

4 cups red new potatoes (unpeeled)

2 medium onions, chopped

2 to 3 Tbsp butter

Salt and pepper to taste

5-6 chicken bouillon cubes

6 cups whole milk

1 cup cream (optional)

Cook potatoes and onions with as little water as possible. When thoroughly cooked, add butter, salt, pepper, and bouillon cubes. Cook together until cubes are dissolved. Mash very fine. Add milk and stir thoroughly. Allow to slowly come to a boil. Add cream and serve immediately.

Main Dishes

Mexican Lasagna

Submitted by Sherry Jacks

2 pounds ground beef
1 can (16 ounces) refried beans
1 can (4 ounces) chopped green chilies
1 envelope taco seasoning
1 Tablespoons hot salsa
12 ounces uncooked lasagna noodles
4 cups shredded Colby-Monterey Jack cheese, divided
1 jar (16 ounces) mild salsa
1/2 cup water
2 cups (16 ounces) sour cream
1 can (2¼ ounces) sliced ripe olives, drained
3 green onions, chopped
1 medium tomato, chopped (optional)

Directions:

1. Preheat oven to 350 degrees. In a large skillet, cook beef over medium heat until no longer pink; drain. Stir in beans, chilies, taco seasoning and hot salsa.

2. In a greased 13x9 inch baking dish, layer a third of the noodles and meat mixture. Sprinkle with 1 cup of cheese. Repeat layers twice.

3. Combine mild salsa and water, pour over top. Cover and bake 1 hour or until heated through.

4. Top with sour cream, olives, onions, tomatoes if desired and remaining cheese. Bake uncovered 5 minutes. Let stand 10-15 minutes before cutting. *Yield: 12 servings.*

Chicken Enchilada Casserole

Submitted by Wanda Strange

Tortilla Chips
3-4 chicken breasts
1 Tbsp. Olive or Vegetable oil
1 can cream of chicken soup
Salsa (desired mild, medium, hot to your family's taste)
2 cups shredded cheese (cheddar or Mexican blend)
  Directions:
  Crush a layer of tortilla chips in the bottom of 9x13 baking dish. Cube Chicken into bite-sized pieces. In a frying pan, heat oil and add the cubed chicken. Layer cooked chicken over the crushed tortilla chips. In a mixing bowl mix the soup and one soup can of the salsa. Pour mixture over the chicken. Cover with cheese. Bake at 350 degrees for 30 minutes or until bubbly.

Jalapeno Chicken Casserole

Submitted by LaNell McNaughten

4 chicken breasts
1/2 t garlic powder
8 oz cream cheese – softened
5-6 jalapeno peppers
4 oz cheddar cheese – grated
½ C crumbled crispy bacon
  Preheat oven to 350 degrees. Lay chicken flat in casserole pan. Season with garlic powder and spread cream cheese over them evenly. Slice peppers thinly and lay on top of cream cheese. Sprinkle cheddar cheese over the top. Bake until done.

Mexican Chicken

Recipe and story submitted by Renee Gresham

Wanda Jaques was a member of our church for many years. She and her husband, Dan raised their two boys in the Bluff Dale Community. For years, our church had fifth Sunday fellowship, which consisted of a potluck dinner after church on the fifth Sunday. Women brought enough food for their families and extra for the visitors who were invited to stay for lunch. Wanda was one of the women who faithfully cooked for fifth Sunday. She always brought the same casserole that came to be known as Wanda's casserole.

Several months ago, I was the recipient of that casserole. Wanda's granddaughter, Jamie, made it for me. She knew I would remember it. She said she hoped it brought me comfort and happy memories. It did!

Here is that recipe.

1 fryer chicken
2 Tbsp butter
1 onion, chopped
Cheese Doritos
Cheese
1 can Ro-Tel tomatoes and green chilies
1 can cream of mushroom soup

Boil and debone chicken. Sauté onion in butter. Add soup and Ro-Tel tomatoes. Use some chicken broth to moisten. Add chicken and simmer a few minutes. Layer Doritos, chicken and cheese in pan. Repeat. Bake at 350 degrees until cheese melts.

Best Ever Meat Loaf

Submitted by Judy Warden

After trying MANY meat loaf recipes, this is our favorite.
The horseradish gives it a nice flavor.
GLAZE:
½ C ketchup
3 T brown sugar
2 T horseradish
2 tsp mustard (regular or spicy)
Combine and set aside
MEAT LOAF:
2 lbs. ground beef
¾ C oats, uncooked
1 large onion, quartered
½ C ketchup
¼ C milk
2 eggs
1 tsp salt
¼ tsp pepper
1 ½ tsp mustard (regular or spicy)
1 T horseradish
Mix beef and oats. Mix rest in blender; then mix with meat mixture.
Spread half of glaze over meat loaf and bake 45 minutes at 375º .
Spread rest of glaze and bake 20 minutes more.
Serves 8.

"Life is too short to eat boring food."
Unknown

Super Duper Nachos

Frances Rhoades
Submitted by her daughter-in-law, Cheryl Rhoades

1 ½ lbs. lean ground beef
1 large onion, chopped
1 large and 1 small can refried beans (Old El Paso)
1 4 oz can diced green chilies
2-3 cups shredded cheddar cheese
¾ cup Taco Sauce
Salt to taste
Dash of Tabasco Sauce
Round Tortilla chips
Garnish with ¼ cup green onions and 1 cup slice black olives

Brown hamburger meat and onion. Discard fat. Season with salt and tabasco to taste. In a 13x9 casserole dish spread the refried beans. Pour hamburger and onion on top. Then spread green chilies and taco sauce. Top with cheese. Bake uncovered at 400 degrees for 30 minutes.

Garnish with green onion and black olives. Serve with chips.

Marinated Chicken Breasts

Submitted by Judy Warden

½ cup soy sauce (I use Kikkoman lite.)
½ cup orange or pineapple juice
¼ cup salad oil
1 teaspoon dry mustard
1 tablespoon firmly packed brown sugar
1 teaspoon ground ginger

1 teaspoon garlic powder
½ teaspoon cracked pepper
1 bunch cilantro (optional)
4-6 meaty, boneless, skinless chicken breasts

Combine all ingredients and put chicken breasts and marinade in a gallon Ziplock bag. Lay bag flat in the refrigerator making sure each chicken breast is soaking in the marinade. Marinate for at least 24 hours, turning once to ensure both sides are thoroughly soaked. The longer you marinate, the juicier the grilled chicken will be. Discard marinade and grill as desired.

Serving suggestion:
Spinach/apple/pecan curry salad
Jasmine rice
Sauteed mushrooms and green onions

Lemon Chicken

From the kitchen of Marionell Frizzell
Submitted to "Meals and Memories"

This makes its own gravy.
4 boneless, skinless chicken breasts halves
½ cup flour
1 can chicken broth
¼ cup lemon juice
Lemon pepper seasoning
Vegetable oil

Sprinkle chicken with lemon pepper and dip into flour. Add just enough oil to a large skillet to cover the bottom. Heat over medium-high heat. Lightly brown the chicken in the hot oil. Remove breasts from pan and add the remaining flour (use more if needed) to hot oil. Stir together, then add the broth and lemon juice, stirring well again. Return the chicken to the skillet and cover with a lid. Simmer for 30 minutes or until chicken is tender.

Crunchy Sausage Casserole

Submitted by LaNell McNaughten

1 pkg log grain wild rice mix
1 lb ground sausage
1 lb ground meat
1 large onion, chopped
1 (8 oz) can water chestnuts, drained
1 can (2 ¾ oz) mushrooms
3 Tbs soy sauce

Cook rice mixture according to directions. Set aside. Cook sausage, ground meat and onion in large skillet, drain. Add rice, water chestnuts, mushrooms and soy sauce, stirring well. Spoon into greased 2-quart casserole dish. Bake uncovered at 325 degrees for 50 minutes.

Sunshine Pudding (A Breakfast Casserole)

Submitted by LaNell McNaughten

1 lb sausage
1 dozen eggs, beaten
1 c milk
Salt and pepper to taste
Buttered bread slices with the crust removed
½ lb Cheddar cheese

Night before serving: Crumble and fry sausage until almost done. Drain on paper towels. Line 9 X 13-inch baking dish with buttered bread slices. Mix sausage, milk, salt, and pepper. Pour over bread. Top with shredded cheese. Cover and put in refrigerator overnight.

Bake until done about 35 minutes just before serving. It's great for company.

Given to LaNell McNaughten by Barb Venable

Breakfast Casserole

Submitted by Cynthia Brown
Shared with Cynthia by Stacy Burch

Crescent Rolls (regular, fat free, or reduced fat) spread in 9x13 greased pan.
Sausage, cooked and spread over rolls. Layer cheddar cheese.
6 eggs, beaten with 1/3 cup milk. Pour over sausage.
Bake at 350 degrees for 30-40 minutes.

Hamburger Pie

Submitted by Carol Richey

1 lb ground beef, cooked and drained
1 can green beans
1 can tomato soup
1 pie crust
Combine first 3 ingredients and pour into pie shell.
Bake at 350 degrees until pie crust is done and filling is heated throughout.

"The only thing better than talking about food is eating it."

John Walters

Granny's Gumbo

Submitted by Cheryl Barron

4 C. boiled, deveined shrimp
1 lb. fresh okra
3 T. bacon drippings (I use olive oil!)
1 cup each: chopped onion, celery, bell pepper
2 sm. or 1 lg. can whole peeled tomatoes
1 14 oz. can chicken broth
1 can water (or more chicken broth)
1 T. salt
1/8 t. pepper
½ t. thyme
2 med. Bay leaves (whole)

In a large heavy Dutch oven over medium heat, add bacon drippings and okra, stirring often. Cook 10-15 minutes. Add onion, celery and bell pepper. Cook 10-15 minutes, stirring often. Add tomatoes, turn heat to low and simmer until the okra quits roping. Add chicken broth, water, salt, pepper, thyme and bay leaves. Continue to simmer on low 1 hour. Add cooked shrimp (and/or chicken) and cook 20 minutes longer. Remove bay leaves before serving. *Serves 8 over cooked rice.*

Chicken Pot Pie

Submitted by Cheryl Barron

2 cans cream of potato soup
1 can drained Veg-All vegetables
2 C. cooked, diced chicken
½ C. milk

½ t. thyme
½ t. black pepper
2 deep dish pie crust shells, thawed
1 egg, slightly beaten

Combine soup, vegetables, chicken, milk, thyme and pepper. Pour into deep dish pie crust. Cover with other crust. Brush crust with slightly beaten egg. Bake 40 minutes at 375.

"Cooking is like love. It should be entered into with abandon or not at all."

Harriet Van Horne

Sloppy Joe

Submitted by Renee Schott

1-pound browned ground beef
1 cup Ketchup
¼ cup water
1 Tbs. brown sugar
2 tsp Worcestershire sauce
1 tsp mustard
½ tsp garlic powder
½ tsp onion powder
½ tsp salt
Hamburger buns

Cook beef – drain. Stir in Ketchup, water, brown sugar, Worcestershire, mustard, garlic and onion powder, and salt. Bring to a boil. Simmer 30-40 minutes. Serve on hamburger buns.

Chicken and Dressing Casserole

Submitted by Renee Schott

4 cups cornbread crumbled (2 boxes of Jiffy)
4 large chicken breasts (cooked and cubed)
1 can cream of mushroom soup
½ tsp poultry seasoning
4 eggs (boiled and chopped)
1 small onion (chopped)
½ tsp pepper
1 stalk celery (diced)
2 cups chicken broth
2 Tbsp melted butter
¼ tsp salt

Combine all ingredients in a bowl and pour into a 9x13-inch lightly greased casserole dish. Bake at 350 degrees for 40-50 minutes or until set.

I had been in the Robinett Family for a very long time before they shared this recipe with me. I found this odd considering I was the favorite daughter-in-law. They told me they cooked it all the time, but this was the first time I had been served the dish and thought it was very good. It reminded me of my Aunt Jean's Chicken Tetrazzini and has become one of my favorites. One is hamburger and the other is chicken. This is one of those recipes you can add whatever to it and it's still um-mmm good!

Terri Robinett

Robinett Family Casserole

From the Kitchen of Terri Robinett
Submitted to "Meals and Memories"

1½ lbs hamburger
    2 carrots, diced
    2 green onions, diced
    3 green peppers, diced
    1 can sliced black olives
    1 can cream of mushroom soup
    1 large can tomatoes
    1 lb spaghetti
    ½ lb Velveeta cheese
    Garlic powder, salt and pepper to taste
    Brown hamburger, drain. Add carrots, onions, peppers, soup, olives, and tomatoes and simmer until carrots are done. Add Velveeta and let melt in hot mixture. Cook spaghetti and mix together with meat mixture. Put in greased casserole dish, put some cheese on top and bake at 350 degrees until it bubbles.

Tater-Tot Casserole

Submitted by Cheryl McCormich Rhoades

Preheat oven to 400 degrees and grease a shallow 2-quart baking dish
    Brown ½ cup frozen chopped onions. 1/3 cup thinly sliced celery, and 1 pound ground beef in a skillet over medium heat. Spoon off any fat. Add salt and pepper to taste. Spread mixture in baking dish. Pour 1 can cream of celery soup over everything. Top with a layer of tater tots.
    Bake 45 minutes or until bubbly.

The History of Aprons
Author Unknown

I don't think most kids today know what an apron is. The principal use of Mom's or Grandma's apron was to protect the dress underneath, because she only had a few. It was also because it was easier to wash aprons than dresses, and aprons used less material. But along with that, it served as a potholder for removing hot pans from the oven. It was wonderful for drying children's tears, and on occasion, was even used for cleaning out dirty ears.

From the chicken coop, the apron was used for carrying eggs, fussy chicks, and sometimes, half-hatched eggs to be finished in the warming oven. When company came, those aprons were ideal hiding places for shy kids. And when the weather was cold, she wrapped it around her arms. Those big old aprons wiped many a perspiring brow, bent over the hot wood stove. Chips and kindling wood were brought into the kitchen in that apron. From the garden, it carried all sorts of vegetables. After the peas had been shelled, it carried out the hulls. In the fall, the apron was used to bring in apples that had fallen from the trees.

When unexpected company drove up the road, it was surprising how much that old apron could dust in a manner of seconds. When dinner was ready, she walked out on the porch, waved her apron, and the men folk knew it was time to come in from the fields to dinner.

It will be a long time before someone invents something that will replace that 'old-time apron' that served so many purposes. Moms and Grandmas used to set hot baked pies on the windowsill to cool. Her granddaughters set theirs on the windowsill to thaw.

They would go crazy now trying to figure out how many germs were on that apron. I don't think I ever caught anything from an apron—but love.

Mom's Meatloaf

Allene McCormick
Submitted to "Meals and Memories"

2 eggs
¾ cup milk
2/3 finely crushed saltine crackers
½ onion chopped
1 tsp salt
Dash of pepper
1½ lbs lean ground beef
Sauce:
1 cup ketchup
½ tsp sage
½ cup packed brown sugar
1 tsp Worcestershire sauce

Beat eggs in a large bowl. Add milk, crackers, onion, salt and pepper. Mix beef into egg mixture. Add half the sauce, mixing well. Shape into 8½ x 4½ inch loaf and place in a shallow baking pan. Spread remaining sauce mixture over the top of the meatloaf and bake at 350 degrees for 60-65 minutes or until no pink remains. Drain. Let stand 10 minutes before serving.

Recipe Recollections

Submitted by Nelda Estes

On hearing about our 150ᵗʰ celebration and the collection of recipes with stories, my mind immediately went to my go to recipe I titled Beef Burgundy ala Nelda. Memories of occasions I served this dish to friends, family and new acquaintances flooded my mind. Unfortunately, the most important memory, the time it was connected to Bluff Baptist failed to materialize. However, thanks to Sherry Jacks and Wanda Strange the recipe and story merged in time to meet the deadline.

I had completely forgotten about our long-ago ministry of fellowship, Dinners for Eight. Carol Richey randomly assigned four couples each quarter and appointed an organizer for each group. It was up to the chosen hostess to determine if the meal would be in her home or at a restaurant.

My first time as hostess, I chose my home because I wanted to serve this recipe. The four couples for that night were Ken and Sherry Slate, Grace and Tom Shelhimer, Jason and Sherry Jacks, Tom and I. The Slates were unable to come that night. Sherry Jacks insisted on bringing dessert as I was taking care of the rest of the menu. I always serve the same side dishes with this recipe, not only because the tastes go well, but mostly because the colors on the plate look great. We eat with our eyes.

Menu:
Beef Burgundy ala Nelda
Steamed Broccoli
Pickled Beets
Buttered Noodles
Toasted Garlic Bread
Dessert

We had such a wonderful time that night. After dinner, the guys ended up in Tom's man cave discussing sports and politics. Us girls, in the family room, discussed endless subjects. I don't think we parted company until three in the morning.

Baptists love to gather around FOOD! We excel in the area of food, fun and fellowship.

Please try this recipe. It is so easy to throw it together and the rewards outweigh the effort. We last had it about three months ago. Please feel free to call me if you have any questions about the recipe.

Beef Burgundy a la Nelda

Submitted by Nelda Estes

2½ - 3 lbs cubed beef
1 package Lipton Onion Soup mix
1 can Campbell's Cream of Mushroom Soup
1 can Campbell's Cream of Chicken Soup
1 can Campbell's Cream of Celery Soup
1 jar boiled small whole onions (may substitute about one cup frozen
    pearl onions
1 jar button mushrooms (may substitute a small can of mushrooms)
1 cup hearty burgundy wine.

Combine all of the proceeding in a large, covered baking dish. Bake at 350 degrees for three hours. Serve over egg noodles.

This dish is even better left over the next day.

"In the childhood memories of every good cook, there's a large kitchen, a warm stove, a simmering pot, and a mom."

Barbara Costikyan

Fresh Texas Venison

Submitted by Cheryl Barron

When my hunting husband gets a deer, the race is on to get the kill back to camp, gutted, skinned, quartered and into a cooler on ice as soon as possible. Even if there's a couple of days left in the hunt, as long as he keeps draining the water and adding more ice, the meat is good. Once he's home, we'll let the meat soak for a couple more days, still adding ice and draining water. The intention is to soak out as much blood as possible, while keeping the meat very cold.

Quartering the deer in the field gives you more time to hunt, meat that's easier to transport, and usually a lower price at the processor, since you've done some of the work. Jeff can do the whole process in about 20 minutes.

We generally order burger (mixed with 10% pork by the processor), butterflied backstrap, tenderloins, tenderized steaks and roasts. Deer is naturally very lean and free of added growth hormones and antibiotics.

I fry up the crumbled burger for tacos, spaghetti sauce, pizzas, nachos, etc. Just add whatever seasoning your dish is leaning toward plus a little water. If you're making hamburger patties, add your preferred seasonings plus more pork sausage (Jimmy Dean's or other) for enough fattiness for the patties to form and hold together.

For the backstrap, t-loins and steaks, I prefer to soak the meat again for 1-2 days, changing the water about every 12 hours to remove more blood. After draining well, I line a 9 X 12 baking dish with the meat, then marinate overnight. Allegro Original Marinade is a favorite. When ready to cook, drain well again, then pan fry or put on the grill. Don't overcook—the meat can dry out.

I serve the steaks, etc. by themselves, or slice for Chinese stir fry, stroganoff, carne asada tacos, etc. I like to cube up the roasts and put in the crock pot for stew.

Hope this encourages you to try some fresh Texas venison!

Crock Pot Brisket

Submitted by Corinne Hopkins

Small Trimmed Brisket (found at HEB)
Liquid Smoke
Bay Leaves
3/4 tsp black pepper
3/4 tsp salt
1 Tbsp chili powder

Mix together pepper, salt and chili powder in small container.
Brush liquid smoke generously on all sides of brisket.
Rub all of the dry seasoning mix on all sides of brisket.
Place brisket on heavy duty foil, fat side up.
Lay bay leaves on top. Wrap up tightly and place in crock pot.
I cook on low for 6 hours. Remove from foil, remove top layer of fat and slice meat against the grain. It will tend to fall apart. If it is tough that means it wasn't cooked long enough.

Note: I have an oblong crock pot. A small brisket wrapped in foil will fit in the bottom tightly. When I have a larger brisket I push it down halfway, add about an extra hour of cooking and it comes out fine.

"Yet he has not left himself without testimony. He has shown kindness by giving you rain from heaven and crops in their seasons; he provides you with plenty of food and fills your heart with joy." (Acts 14:17 NIV)

Mexican Cornbread Casserole

From the kitchen of Geneva Stinson
As submitted to "Meals and Memories"

1 lb lean ground meat browned and drained
½ cup chopped onion
3 or 4 jalapeno peppers, chopped
2 medium eggs, beaten
2 can (15 oz each) cream style corn
½ cup milk
1 package (6.5 oz) cornbread mix
4-6 slices American or cheddar cheese

    Heat oven to 450 degrees. Put meat, onions and jalapenos together, set aside. Combine beaten eggs, milk, and 1 can cream style corn with the dry cornbread mix. Stir until all the ingredients are moistened. Pour half of batter into a 9x9x2 inch deep pan. Top with beef-onion-pepper mixture, cheese and remaining corn. Pour remaining batter over top and bake 25-30 minutes, until golden brown and done.

Vegetable and Side Dishes

Fresh Squash Casserole

Submitted by E & R Fudge & Co

3 cups zucchini or yellow squash, sliced
¼ cup onion, chopped
4 Tbsp. margarine
2 eggs beaten
¼ cup milk
½ tsp. salt
½ tsp. pepper
1 cup sharp cheddar cheese grated
1 cup Ritz crackers, crushed
Preheat oven to 350 degrees. Sauté squash and onions in margarine until tender. Drain. Add remaining ingredients except cheese and crackers. Spoon into a 9x13-inch greased dish. Top with cheese and crackers. Bake 20 minutes.

Broccoli Casserole

Previously submitted by Lou Stone to the Paluxy Valley Cookbook

¼ cup chopped onions
¼ cup chopped celery
1 (10 ounce) package frozen broccoli
2 cups cooked rice
1 can mushroom soup
1 (8 ounce) jar Cheez Whiz
   Mix all ingredients in a large bowl. Pour into buttered casserole dish. Bake 45 minutes at 350 degrees.

Lou Stone's Spanish Rice

Submitted by Renee Gresham

I make this recipe every time we have Mexican food at our house.

1 Large can stewed tomatoes
1 ½ cups chicken broth
1 ¼ c uncooked rice
1 Tbsp butter
2 tsp chili powder
¾ tsp oregano
½ tsp garlic salt

In medium sauce pan, combine all ingredients. Bring to a boil, reduce the heat. Cover and simmer 25 minutes, or until the rice is done. Garnish with green onions. Serves six.

Squash Casserole

Submitted by Georgia Scott
Previously shared in the Paluxy Valley Cookbook

4 cups squash, cooked and drained
1 cup sour cream
1 medium onion, chopped
1 medium green pepper, chopped (optional)
1 tsp salt
¼ tsp pepper
½ cup water
¼ cup Monterey Jack cheese, grated

Combine all ingredients, except cheese. Cook on medium heat for 20-25 minutes until squash is tender. Garnish with grated cheese.

Corn Casserole

From the Kitchen of Anna Watson
As submitted to "Meals and Memories"

On November 18, 2007, The Sunday before Thanksgiving, Bluff Dale Baptist Church served Thanksgiving Dinner after church. By combining 3 recipes and some experimentation, I came up with the following Corn Casserole. The recipes I used came from Katie Sue Parker, Marionelle Frizzell, and Bille Verne Graves.

1 can (14 ¾ oz) whole kernel corn
1 can (14 ¾ oz) cream style corn
Salt and pepper to taste
1 can (4 oz) green chilis chopped
2 Tbsp oil
½ package Morrison Corn Kits Cornbread mix
8 oz cheddar cheese (save half for topping)
3 eggs beaten

Mix together the first 6 ingredients plus one half the cheese. Add beaten eggs. Bake at 350 degrees until set, about 40-50 minutes. Sprinkle remaining cheese on top and return to oven to brown lightly.

"Laughter is the brightest in the place where the food is."
Irish Proverb

Squash Casserole

**Story and recipe from the kitchen of Marionell Frizzell
As submitted to "Meals and Memories"**

In the spring and summer of 2007, Bluff Dale had lots of rain. We had a small garden behind our garage where we planted eight squash plants and 6 tomato vines. I had added a lot of mulch and fertilizer. The rain kept coming and the squash and tomatoes kept growing. The leaves on the squash were as large as elephant ears, and every other day I gathered a bucketful of squash. I learned a long time ago that squash could be sliced and frozen in plastic bags, later dipped in cornmeal mix, dropped in hot oil, and fried. Although this is very good, there soon becomes more than is needed. I tried several squash casseroles but none that we really liked. Here is a casserole I put together that we like, and other people have asked for the recipe.

1 carton (8 oz) sour cream
1 pkg (4 oz) cream cheese, melted
½ carrot, grated
1 small can mushrooms (optional)
1 can water chestnuts, cut in halves
2 cups squash boiled, drained and mashed
Seasoned breadcrumbs to cover completely

Heat first 5 ingredients together, then add the cooked squash. Stir all together. Spray an 8x8 inch baking dish with vegetable spray. Pour squash mixture into dish and top with breadcrumbs and grated cheese. Bake at 375 degrees just until cheese melts.

Macaroni Mushroom Casserole

Submitted by Sherry Slate
From my American Cooking Cookbook Bought in 1966

Thanksgiving favorite
    *Also known as Texas Comfort in Pennsylvania – served by Abigail
in Reunion, Germany, Luxembourg Crackeroni by Eileen's family*
2 Cups Macaroni (measured raw) Cooked
1 Can Cream of Mushroom Soup
1 Cup Mayo
1 Small Can Mushrooms
¼ Cup of Green Pepper
¼ Cup Onion
1 Small Jar of Pimentos
1 lb. Grated Sharp Cheddar Cheese
1 tsp. Salt
    Mix Cracker Crumbs & Margarine (enough to moisten crackers)
    Mix all ingredients, except cracker crumbs and margarine mixture.
Grease an ovenproof bowl, add casserole and top with cracker crumb
mixture. Cook at 375 degrees for 25 to 30 minutes.

Potatoes — Bobby's Secret Recipe

**Previously shared by Bobby Block in the Paluxy Valley
Cookbook**

Onions
Butter
Soy Sauce
Potatoes cooked and cut up in medium pieces
1 can cream of mushroom soup

Slices of Velveeta Cheese
Milk
Salt and Pepper to taste

Sauté onion in butter and soy sauce. In a casserole dish put cooked potatoes, sauteed onions, cream of mushroom soup, slices of Velveeta cheese, a little milk, and salt and pepper. Finish in microwave.

Fried Cauliflower

From the kitchen of Lou Stone
As submitted to "Meals and Memories"

1 egg
3 Tbsp plain dried breadcrumbs
2 cups small cauliflower florets, blanched and cooled
1 Tbsp vegetable oil
¼ tsp salt
Dash of pepper
Parsley sprigs for garnish

In shallow medium bowl, beat egg lightly. Place breadcrumbs in plastic bag. Dip cauliflower into egg to coat, and then place florets in bag with crumbs. Close bag and shake well. In a 10-inch skillet, heat oil. Add coated cauliflower and sauté until browned on all sides. Season with salt and pepper if desired and serve garnished with parsley snips.

"When one of those at the table with him heard this, he said to Jesus, 'Blessed is the one who will eat at the feast in the kingdom of God.'" (Luke 14:15 NIV).

Sweet Potato Casserole

Previously submitted by Lou Stone to Paluxy Valley Cookbook

1 large can sweet potatoes, drained
2 eggs
¾ cup sugar
1/3 cup Pet canned milk
1 stick butter
1 tsp vanilla

Put all the ingredients in large bowl and mix well. Pour into buttered casserole dish. Top casserole with Crunchy Topping.

1 cup light brown sugar
1/3 cup flour
1/3 cup melted butter
1 cup chopped pecans

Mix well and sprinkle on top of sweet potato casserole. Bake at 350 degrees for 35 minutes.

Sweet Potato Casserole

Story and recipe submitted by Wanda Strange
Previously submitted by Sue Braun to the Paluxy Valley Cookbook

Sue and Dick Braun moved to Bluff Dale from the DFW Metroplex. When we first moved to the community and to BDBC, she shared how much she loved this community. Jokingly she said, "I was so happy to live in this community and was especially impressed that no one talked bad about anyone. Then I found out they were all related."

I look forward to seeing Dick and Sue again, when we all get to heaven. I am submitting the Sweet Potato Casserole in loving memory of this amazing and beautiful woman, with a great sense of style and awesome sense of humor.

3 cups cooked and mashed sweet potatoes

½ cup sugar

¼ cup milk

1/3 cup melted margarine

1 Tbsp vanilla

2 eggs, beaten

1 cup crushed pineapple, drained

Combine above

1 cup flaked coconut

1 cup firmly packed brown sugar

1/3 cup flour

1/3 cup melted margarine

1 cup chopped pecans

Sprinkle over top of sweet potatoes. Bake at 375 degrees for 25 minutes or until golden brown

Puddings, Candy, and More

Bake Sale Auction Star

Bake-sale auctions at BDBC provided a lucrative fund-raising opportunity to send teens to youth camp. Church members paid $$$ for favorite desserts which they sometimes took home but often unwrapped and shared with everyone who wanted a taste. One item consistently stood out as the star of each auction. A plate of Chocolate Chip Cookies sparked a bidding war between Glenda Sargent and Harry Woodward. The bid climbed as neither buyer backed down. Ultimately, Glenda walked away with the prize. Determined not to let Harry win, Glenda kept bidding until Harry finally conceded. Secretly, I suspect he might have feared Veronica's wrath if he kept bidding. Glenda paid a record price of $750 for Anna Watson's cookies, well worth every penny.

Wanda Strange

Jena Banana Pudding

Submitted by Scott and Cindi Pace

1 Large box instant vanilla or banana pudding
1 Can Eagle Brand Milk
1 Carton Cool Whip

Mix pudding with 2 cups milk. Mix in Eagle Brand and Cool Whip.

Layer vanilla wafers, bananas, and pudding mixture.

Lemon Fluff

Judy Warden's Mother's Recipe
Submitted by Judy Warden

This was my mother's recipe, and I make it every Summer. It is so refreshing and easy to make.

CHILL:

- 1 large can PET milk

MIX & COOL:

- 1, 3-oz. pkg. lemon Jello

- ½ c. hot water

- 2 lemons (juice & rind)

MIX and PRESS into oblong PYREX dish (save ½ cup crumbs for top):

- 2 cups graham cracker crumbs

- 2 T sugar

- 1 stick unsalted butter (melted)

Whip PET milk until soft peaks form and add 1 cup sugar. Add cold Jello mixture and mix well.

Pour into oblong Pyrex dish and top with remaining crumbs. ·
Chill 4 to 6 hours.

Serves 12-15

"Gracious words are like honeycomb, sweet to the soul and healing to the bones." (Proverbs 16:24 NIV).

Bread Pudding

Submitted by Nancy Fuller

2/3 loaf sandwich bread (can use 1 package of hamburger or hotdog
   buns) torn into pieces.
2 cups sugar
3 eggs beaten
2 cups milk
1 Tbsp vanilla extract
1 ½ sticks butter
1 tsp cinnamon
Carmel ice cream topping
   Preheat oven to 350 degrees. Melt butter in the oven in a 9x13 pan.
Remove pan from oven and place bread pieces in pan.
   Mix together remaining ingredients and pour over bread.
   Bake 50-60 minutes
   Remove from oven and drizzle with caramel ice cream topping.

Escalloped Pineapple

Submitted by Judy Evans

Simple to make. We all love it.
4 slices day old bread
1 large can crushed pineapple (drained)
1 cup sugar
1 stick butter (or margarine)
1 beaten egg
¼ cup milk
   Mix bread, sugar, eggs, and milk. Add melted butter and beat well.
Add pineapple and mix.
   Bake in casserole dish at 350 degrees for 30 minutes.

Mother's Pudding

Hettie Jackson and Effie Rhoades Harris
Submitted by Cynthia Brown

Sauce:
Mix ¼ cup sugar and 2 Tbsp of cocoa.
Stir in 1/3 cup boiling water until smooth.
Stir in ½ cup evaporated milk
Dough:
Sift:
½ cup flour
1/3 cup sugar
¾ tsp baking powder
2 Tbsp cocoa
1/8 tsp salt
Fold in ½ cup nuts
   Put 2 Tbsp milk, 2 Tbsp water, 2 Tbsp melted shortening, and ½ tsp vanilla in a bowl.
   Mix quickly but thoroughly. Mixture will be thick. Spread in a greased pan.
   Prepare and pour the sauce mixture over the top but don't mix it in. Mix and spread dough over top.
   Bake at 350-degree oven for 20 minutes. Cake should be firm to touch. Serve warm with sauce.
   Double recipe for 4 servings.

Chocolate and Peanut Butter Truffles

Submitted by Sherry Jacks

1 c. Reese's Peanut Butter Chips
¾ c. butter
½ c. Hershey's Cocoa
14 oz. can Eagle Brand sweetened condensed milk
1 Tbs. Vanilla
Coatings: Finely chopped nuts, unsweetened chocolate, graham
cracker crumbs, or confectioner's sugar
   In heavy saucepan, over low heat, melt chips with butter. Stir in
cocoa until smooth. Add sweetened condensed milk and vanilla.
Cook and stir until thickened and well blended, about 4 minutes.
Remove from heat. Chill 2 hours or until firm enough to handle.
Shape into 1-inch balls. Roll in any of the above coatings. Chill
until firm (About one hour) Store covered in fridge.
   This makes about 3 dozen.

Candy

Submitted by Cheryl McCormick Rhoades

1 cup walnuts
1 cup pecans
1 cup salted peanuts
Chocolate bark
   Mix together. Melt Chocolate bark and pour over nut mixture.
Drop by spoonful onto wax paper.

"Taste and see that the Lord is good; blessed is the one who takes refuge in Him." (Psalm 34:8 NIV).

Edd's Mother's Creamy Pecan Pralines

Submitted by Terri Robinett

We make these at Christmas and will give as gifts if there's any left-over!

½ Cup Sugar (set aside)

2 Cups Sugar

2/3 Cup Evaporated Milk

2 Cups Pecans (whole, halved or broken...depends on what you like. We usually will use large broken pieces)

2 Tsp Vanilla

2 Tbsps. Butter

You might need someone to help with this recipe! I always do.

Spray wax paper with Pam or use a cookie sheet sprayed with Pam or butter, set aside until ready to use.

In small heavy skillet over medium heat, caramelize ½ cup sugar until melted, stirring frequently. In the meantime, cook the 2 cups sugar and evaporated milk in a 2-to-3-quart saucepan stirring frequently, making sure the sugar and milk are blended. Add the caramelized sugar and pecans. Cook on medium heat until mixture reaches the soft ball stage when dropped into cold water (236 degree) and then cook a little longer. Add vanilla and butter BUT do not stir! Let cool for about 20 to 30 minutes then stir until it begins to hold shape. Drop into mounds on your prepared wax paper. *Makes about 40 pralines.*

Chocolate Peanut Patties

Submitted by Cynthia Brown

1 bag Reese's morsels
1 bag Milk Chocolate Chips
1 jar non-salted peanuts
  Melt chocolate chips and Resse's morsels in the microwave.
  Add peanuts and stir.
  Drop on cookie sheet and cool.

"God gives us the nuts, but He doesn't crack them."
Franz Kafka

Peanut Patties

Submitted by Cynthia Brown

2½ cups sugar
2/3 cup white Karo syrup
1 small can evaporated milk
3 cups raw peanuts
  Mix together and cook to soft ball stage, stirring constantly
Add:
1 tbsp oleo
1 tsp vanilla
¼ cup powdered sugar
  Beat until creamy.
  Drop by Tbsp on greased wax paper.

Spicy Orange Pecans

Submitted by Sherry Jacks

Ingredients:
1½ cups powdered sugar
2 Tbs. corn starch
1 tsp. cinnamon
¼ tsp. allspice
½ tsp. salt
1 Tbs. grated orange zest (grate just the orange-colored peel)
2 Egg whites slightly beaten
2 Tbs. fresh orange juice
2 cups pecan halves

Preparation:
Sift together sugar, cornstarch, cinnamon, allspice and salt. Stir in the orange zest. In a separate bowl, blend the egg whites and orange juice. Stir the pecans into the egg white mixture, coating completely. Drain thoroughly. Then roll in the sugar mixture, coating well. Spread on a cookie sheet in single layer and not touching. Bake at 250 degrees for 20-25 minutes or until crisp. Cool prior to storing. You can substitute walnuts if you prefer.

Melting Chocolate on the Stove Top
The best way to melt chocolate is on the hob (stove) in either a double boiler or a glass bowl over a pan of simmering water. Though this is way lengthier than melting in a microwave, you will have more control over the melting process and less risk of burning. [1]

---

1. Lemm 2019

Peanut Butter Logs

From the kitchen of Marionell Frizzell
As submitted to "Meals and Memories"

I have a very good friend who lives in Tennessee. She is a very good cook, and I have gotten many recipes from her. This one is a great Christmas sweet.

1 cup peanut butter
1 cup powdered sugar
1 cup chopped walnuts
1 cup chopped dates
4 squares semisweet chocolate, melted
Shredded coconut for rolling

Mix first four ingredients, mixing together like a pastry. Roll dough into a small log. Dip or roll in melted chocolate and then coconut. If dough is too stiff to roll into a log, add a little coffee or milk. Refrigerate. Slice to serve.

Pumpkin Scones

Submitted by Sherry Jacks

Ingredients:
For the Scones
1 cup spelt flour (substitute whole wheat flour)
1 cup all-purpose flour
½ Tbsp. baking powder
½ tsp. ground cinnamon
¼ tsp. ground nutmeg
¼ tsp. ground allspice
¼ tsp. ground ginger

1/8 tsp. ground cloves

1 Tbsp. granulated sugar

1 Tbsp. brown sugar

¼ cup vegan butter (substitute regular butter)

1/3 cup pumpkin puree

1/3 cup almond milk

For the cinnamon icing

¼ cup powdered sugar

½ Tbsp almond milk

Cinnamon and nutmeg to taste

For the Pumpkin Spice Icing

1/2 cup powdered sugar

2 tsp. almond milk

2 tsp. pumpkin puree

Cinnamon and ground cloves to taste

Instructions:
For the scones

1. Mix together dry ingredients

2. Cut in cold butter. If your dough gets too warm at any point, stick it in the fridge.

3. Stir in milk and pumpkin puree.

4. Mix until ball of dough forms. You'll likely need to use your hands as it will be dry at first.

5. Roll dough into rectangle. Slice into triangles

6. Bake at 375 degrees for 12 minutes

For the Icing

Mix all ingredients together. Adjust amount of milk to achieve desired thickness.

Glazed Mixed Nuts

Submitted by Sherry Jacks

Ingredients:
1 Egg white slightly beaten
2 TBS cold water
2/3 cup Walnut halves
2/3 cup Pecan halves
2/3 cup Whole Almonds
½ cup sugar
1½ tsp cinnamon
¼ tsp ground ginger
¼ tsp ground nutmeg
Preparation:
   Beat egg white and water until frothy. Stir nuts into mixture to coat and drain slightly in colander. (3-4 minutes) Mix sugar and spices in a bag. Add nuts and shake until coated. Spread in a single layer on a microwave safe plate/platter. Microwave on high for 1½ minutes or until bubbly. Stir. Microwave another 1½ minutes. Remove. Separate. Cool. Store or serve.

Orange Tea Muffins

Submitted by E & R Fudge & Co.

2 cups sugar, divided
½ cup fresh orange juice

½ cup butter or margarine softened
¾ cup sour cream
2 cups flour
1 tsp baking soda
1 tsp salt
1 tsp grated orange peel
½ cup raisins
½ cup chopped nuts

    Combine 1 cup sugar and the orange juice. Set aside.
    Cream butter and remaining sugar; blend in sour cream.
    Combine dry ingredients and add to the creamed mixture.
    Beat at low just until all ingredients are combined.
    Stir in orange peel, raisins and nuts.
    The batter will be stiff.
    Spoon batter into 1¾ cup muffin tins, filling each cup completely full.
    Bake at 375 degrees for about 12 minutes or until done.
    While still warm, dip each muffin in sugar/orange mixture.
    Cool on wire rack.
    Yield 36 small muffins.

Grandmother's Frosting

Submitted by Cynthia Brown

White Cake, Yellow Cake, Any Cake
½ stick butter
½ cup brown sugar
¼ cup milk
Powdered sugar

    Melt butter in saucepan. Add brown sugar and boil for a few minutes. Add milk. Sift powdered sugar and combine with other ingredients. Pour over cake.

Birthday Icing

From the Kitchen of Ella Matthews
As submitted by Cynthia Brown

½ cup corn syrup
¾ cup sugar
¼ cup water
   Cook together until spins a thread
   Pour over 3 stiff egg whites and beat until fluffy.
   Add ½ tsp cream of tartar and 1 tsp vanilla.

Six Weeks Raisin Muffins

Submitted by Cynthia Brown

1 15-ounce box Raisin Bran
1 cup vegetable oil
3 cups sugar
4 eggs beaten
1 quart buttermilk
2 cups flour sifted
2 tsp soda
2 tsp salt
   Mix bran, sugar, flour, soda and salt together in a large bowl.
   Add beaten eggs, oil and milk.
   Fill muffin tins 2/3 full.
   Bake at 400 degrees for 15-20 minutes.
   Batter may be stored, covered in the refrigerator for up to six weeks.

Applesauce Nut Bread

Submitted by LaNell McNaughten

2 C Sugar
1 C applesauce
1/3 C vegetable oil
2 eggs
3 Tbs Milk
2 C flour
1 tsp soda
½ tsp baking powder
½ tsp cinnamon
¼ tsp salt
¼ tsp nutmeg
1 C pecans, divided
2 Tbs brown sugar
½ tsp cinnamon

Combine first 5 ingredients in large mixing bowl. Beat at medium speed for 1 minute. Set aside. Combine next 6 ingredients. Add to applesauce mixture. Beat until smooth. Stir in ¾ C pecans.

Spoon Batter into a greased floured 9X5X3" loaf pan.

Combine remaining pecans, brown sugar and cinnamon. Sprinkle over batter and bake at 350 F for 30 minutes. Remove from oven and cover loosely with foil. Return to oven for 40 additional minutes. Uncover and cool 10 minutes in pan. Remove from pan and cool on wire rack.

Lemon Nut Bread

Submitted by LaNell McNaughten

1/3 cup butter, melted
1 ¼ cup sugar
2 eggs
¼ tsp almond extract
1 ½ cup flour
1 tsp baking powder
1 tsp salt
½ cup milk
1 Tbs lemon rind, grated
3 Tbs lemon juice
½ cup chopped nuts (optional)

Glaze:
3 Tbs lemon juice
1/4 cup powdered sugar

Cream butter & sugar. Add eggs one at a time, Stir in extract. Mix flour with salt and baking powder. Add flour mixture alternately with milk to butter and sugar. Fold in lemon rind and 3 Tbs lemon juice and nuts. Bake in greased loaf pan 70 minutes at 325 degrees.

Mix remaining lemon juice and powdered sugar. Spoon mixture over hot loaf. Puncture with a toothpick to allow glaze to soak in. Cool for 10 minutes before removing from pan.

"She gets up while it is still night; she provides food for her family and portions for her female servants." (Proverbs 31:15 NIV).

Chocolate Cheesecake

Submitted by E & R Fudge Co

Heat oven to 450 degrees

Crust:

Combine 1 cup chocolate wafer crumbs and ¼ cup (1/2 stick) butter or margarine; press into bottom of 9" spring form pan. To easily crush chocolate wafer cookies, place them in a sealed plastic food storage bag and press with a rolling pin.

Filling:

3 packages cream cheese, softened

1 ¼ Cups sugar

1 (8 ounce) container of sour cream

2 tsp vanilla

½ cup cocoa

2 Tbs flour

3 Eggs

Beat cream cheese and sugar until blended. Add sour cream and vanilla. Beat until blended. Beat in cocoa and flour. Add eggs one at a time, beat just until blended. Pour into crust. Bake 10 minutes. Reduce oven temperature to 250 degrees. Continue baking 40 minutes. Remove from oven to wire rack. With knife, loosen from the side of the pan. Cool completely. Remove side of the pan.

Tip: Check cheesecake for doneness by gently shaking the pan. If it's set except for small jiggly area in the center, it is done.

Chocolate drizzle

Place ½ cup semi-sweet chocolate chips and 2 tsp shortening (do not use butter, margarine, spread or oil) in a small microwave safe bowl. Microwave at High (100%) for 30 seconds. If necessary, microwave at high, stirring after each heating, just until chips are melted. Drizzle over the top of the cheesecake.

Refrigerate for 4-6 hours. Store covered in the refrigerator.

Serves 12

Sopapilla Cheesecake

Submitted by LaNell McNaughten

2 cans Crescent Rolls
2-8oz packages of cream cheese
1 Cup sugar
Topping:
½ Cup sugar (for topping)
1 stick butter
Cinnamon to taste

Preheat oven to 350 degrees. Spray 9X13 baking dish with cooking spray. Roll out 1 can crescent rolls in bottom of pan, do not separate, just roll out in rectangle to cover bottom of dish. Mix both packages of cream cheese and 1 cup sugar. Mix well. Spread mixture over crescent rolls in pan then add last can crescent rolls on top. Pour melted stick of butter over top layer of rolls then top with remaining ½ cup sugar and cinnamon. Bake for approximately 30 minutes. Time may vary. Cook until top is golden brown, and center is well done.

Gingerbread

Submitted by E & R Fudge & Co

Spicy and rich – best served warm
1 ½ Cups flour
½ tsp salt
½ tsp baking powder
½ tsp baking soda
¾ tsp cinnamon
¾ tsp ginger

½ tsp allspice

½ cup shortening

½ cup boiling water

½ cup firmly packed brown sugar

½ cup dark molasses

1 egg slightly beaten

Combine flour, salt, baking powder, soda, cinnamon, ginger, all-spice. Set aside.

Combine shortening, boiling water in a large bowl. Blend in brown sugar, molasses and egg. Gradually add dry ingredients.

Pour batter into an 8- or 9-inch square pan. Bake at 350 degrees for 30-40 minutes or until wooden pick inserted in the center comes out clean. Serve with sweetened whipped cream, spiced applesauce, or "tangy lemon sauce".

Serves 9-12

Cakes

Easy Chocolate Bundt Cake

Submitted by Cheryl McCormick Rhoades

1 box chocolate cake mix
1 3.9 ounce box chocolate pudding mix
1 cup sour cream
1 cup vegetable oil
4 eggs
½ cup warm water
1 cup chocolate chips (optional)
Heat oven to 350 degrees. Combine all ingredients and mix until well blended. DO NOT OVER MIX. Spray bundt pan and pour in batter. Bake 50-60 minutes or until toothpick comes out clean.
Glaze:
¼ cup sugar
3 Tbsp. cocoa
3 Tbsp. milk
1 Tbsp. Butter
   Place all ingredients into saucepan over medium heat, stir to combine. After combining DO NOT STIR AGAIN. After it boils and has formed bubbles, remove from heat. Let it cool one minute and pour over cake. Sprinkle with chocolate or colored sprinkles.

Pear Cake

Submitted by Carol Richey

2 cups sugar
¾ cup oil
1 tsp cinnamon
1 tsp ginger

Pinch of cloves

3 cups finely chopped pears (I use a food processor)

2 eggs

1 cup chopped pecans

1 tsp soda

1 tsp salt

3 cups flour

Mix all ingredients and spoon into greased and floured pan(s).

Hint: You can also use apples.

Bake at 350 degrees about 30 minutes for muffins or about 60 minutes for a bundt pan.

Moist Pound Cake

Submitted by Sherry Jacks

4 eggs

2 c. sugar

1 c. margarine

3 c. flour

½ tsp. soda

1 tsp. baking powder

1 tsp. vanilla

1 tsp. lemon extract

1 c. sour milk or buttermilk

Mix all together and bake in square cake pan at 325 degrees for 60 minutes or until done.

Sock It to Me Cake

Submitted by Cynthia Brown

Cake:
1 package yellow (or butter) cake mix
1 cup sour cream
½ cup oil
¼ cup sugar
¼ cup water
4 eggs
Filling:
1 cup chopped pecans
1 tsp cinnamon
2 Tbsp brown sugar
2 Tbsp reserved cake mix
   Preheat oven to 375 degrees.
   Blend cake mix, sour cream, oil, sugar, water and eggs.
   Beat at high speed for 2 minutes.
   Pour 2/3 of the batter in bundt pan.
   Combine filling ingredients and sprinkle over batter in the pan.
   Spread remaining batter over filling mixture.
   Bake at 375 degrees for 45-55 minutes.
Glaze:
1 cup confectioner's sugar
2 Tbsp milk

*"After David had finished sacrificing the burnt offerings
and fellowship offerings, he blessed the people in the name
of the Lord. Then he gave a loaf of bread, a cake of dates
and a cake of raisins to each Israelite man and woman."
(1 Chronicles 16:2-3 NIV).*

Texas So Good Cake

Submitted by LaNell McNaughten

1 box German chocolate cake mix (with pudding)
   1 pkg craft caramels
   1 14 oz can sweetened condensed milk
   1 pkg chocolate chips
   2 sticks butter
   1 cup or bag of chopped pecans
Prepare cake mix according to directions. Divide batter in half. Into first half add 1 stick butter (melted) and add ½ cup eagle brand milk. Pour into greased 13 X 9" pan. Bake 30 minutes at 325 F

About 5 minutes before removing from oven, melt caramels, 1 stick butter and balance of eagle brand milk in microwave. Pour over cake. Sprinkle chocolate chips and pecans on the cake. Pour rest of batter over this and bake 30 minutes at 325 F or until done.

Weight Watchers Pineapple Angel Food Cake

Submitted by Wanda Strange

1 box Angel Food Cake Mix
1 20-oz can crushed pineapple
In large bowl, mix together the cake mix and pineapple (do not drain)

Pour into a greased bundt or tube pan. Bake at 350 degrees approximately 50-60 minutes or until a toothpick comes out clean.

Aunt Opal's Chocolate Buttermilk Cake

Story and Recipe
Submitted by LaNell McNaughten.

All of our family loved Aunt Opal's Buttermilk Cake, but no one could create the tasty dessert to compare to her cake. When she died, the nieces all fought over her cake pan as they were convinced the pan was the missing component. My mother won the pan and made the dessert for almost every event. As she grew older, she forgot the pan was Aunt Opal's coveted pan and threw it away. I never had the heart to tell her cousins what happened to the pan.

2 C sugar
2 C flour
1 tsp soda
1 tsp cinnamon
1 C water
1 stick margarine
½ C oil
4 TBS cocoa
2 eggs
1 tsp vanilla
½ C buttermilk

Mix first 4 ingredients together and set aside. Put next 4 ingredients in saucepan and melt together. Bring to a boil and pour over dry ingredients. Mix well. Mix eggs, vanilla, and buttermilk together and pour with chocolate mixture. Bake at 400 F for 20 minutes.

Chocolate Icing for Buttermilk Cake

1 ½ stick margarine
6 TBS cocoa
9 TBS buttermilk
¾ bag of powdered sugar
1 tsp salt

2 tsp vanilla

1 C pecans (optional)

Place margarine, cocoa and milk in saucepan and bring to a boil. Add powdered sugar, vanilla and pecans. Ice cake while the cake is still hot. Puncture the cake with a toothpick to allow icing to soak into the cake.

P.S. The cake tastes just like Aunt Opal's if you use a 10 X 15" jelly roll pan. So, the pan was the key.

Coconut Pound Cake

Jean Tucker's recipe
Submitted by her cousin, Cynthia Brown

1 cup Crisco

2 cups sugar

5 eggs

1 cup buttermilk

2 cups flour

1½ tsp baking powder

1 tsp salt

1 tsp coconut extract

1 small can Angel Flake coconut.

Cream sugar and Crisco together. Add eggs one at a time and beat for exactly two minutes after each. Add remaining ingredients. Bake in a tube pan (sprayed with Pam) at 375 degrees for 50-60 minutes until done.

Glaze:

1 cup sugar

½ cup water

1 tsp coconut extract

Mix all glaze ingredients and pour over cake.

Apricot Nectar Cake

Submitted by Sherry Slate
Obtained from Dorothy Monroe

A family and friend favorite...Kerry Strange, this one's for you!
1 box Duncan Hines Lemon Supreme cake mix
¾ c. Crisco oil
1 c. apricot nectar
½ c. sugar
4 eggs

   Mix oil, nectar, sugar, and cake mix at low speed. Add eggs one at a time and mix well after each addition. Pour into Bundt pan. Bake at 325 for 1hr. Cool for 10 min. Invert onto plate.
Glaze: 1 c. sugar and juice of 2 lemons.

   Drizzle or pour over cake...I brush this on while the cake is very hot so it will be absorbed into it.

Adrian's Fluffy Tres Leches Cake

Adrian Saucedo
Submitted by Melissa Saucedo

Pre-heat oven to 350.
   Butter a 9x13 casserole dish.
Sift:
1 C All-Purpose flour
1 1/2 tsp baking powder
1/4 tsp salt
Beat:
5 egg whites (beat at high speed until soft peaks form, appx. 1 min.)
slowly add 1/4C sugar (stiff peaks but not dry, appx. 1 min.)

<u>Beat:</u> (in a separate bowl)
5 egg yolks
3/4 C sugar
(once the color is a pale yellow) stir in;
1/3 C milk
1 tsp vanilla

Pour yolk mixture over dry ingredients. Mix with spatula then fold egg white mixture until combined. Pour into casserole dish and bake for 25-30 min. Once cooked, when toothpick comes out clean, set out to cool completely. Keep in a secured temp. area (outside air can cause the cake to flatten in certain areas and become uneven).

<u>Meanwhile, Mix: (Milk Mixture)</u>
12 oz evaporated milk
9 oz sweetened condensed milk
1/3 C heavy whipping cream

Once cake has cooled, poke tiny holes all over with a toothpick. Slowly drizzle the above milk mixture over the cake. Let the milk mixture soak into the holes and the cake rest for 30 min. Top with homemade whipped cream and strawberries. Tip: Refrigerate leftovers for breakfast with coffee.

But he continued, "You are from below; I am from above. You are of this world; I am not of this world. I told you that you would die in your sins; if you do not believe that I, am he, you will indeed die in your sins. "Who are you?" they asked.
"Just what I have been telling you from the beginning," Jesus replied. "I have much to say in judgment of you. But he who sent me is trustworthy, and what I have heard from him I tell the world."
They did not understand that he was telling them about his Father. So Jesus said, "When you have lifted up the Son of Man, then you will know that I am he and that I do nothing on my own but speak just what the Father has taught me. (John 8:23-28 NIV).

Cream Cheese Pound Cake

Aunt Rosie's Recipe
Submitted by Cynthia Brown

All ingredients need to be room temperature
1½ cup butter
1 8-ounce package cream cheese
1½ cup sugar
1/3 cup sour cream
1 tsp vanilla
6 large eggs
3 cups cake flour
½ tsp baking powder
1/8 tsp salt
   Beat butter for 2 minutes
   Scrape sides. Add cream cheese. Beat one minute.
   Add sugar. Beat one minute.
   Add sour cream and vanilla. Beat until combined.
   Beat each step on high
   On low speed, add eggs one at a time, fully mixing before adding
each egg.
   Add flour, baking powder, and salt. Beat on medium until combined.
   Bake 75-90 minutes. Toothpick inserted should come out clean.
   Allow to sit in pan to cool. Turn out. *YUM!*

"Older women are the secret of the best cakes."
Franklin D. Roosevelt

Lemon Apricot Pound Cake

Submitted by Elayne Block

Duncan Hines Butter Cake Mix
¾ cup Apricot nectar
¾ cup oil
1 small package lemon Jello
2 Tbsp lemon extract
4 eggs
  Combine all ingredients and beat 3 minutes.
  Spray pan (Bundt or loaf) with Pam.
  Bake at 325 degrees for 1 hour.

Glaze:
¾ powdered sugar
1 Tbsp milk

Irish Apple Cake

Submitted by Renee Schott

1½ Cup Wesson Oil
2 cups sugar
1 tsp baking soda
1 tsp cinnamon
1 Cup Nuts
2 eggs
3 cups all-purpose flour
½ tsp salt
3 cups raw apples, peeled and diced
  Combine all of the ingredients.
  Pour batter into a Bundt or tube pan.
  Bake at 350 degrees for 40 minutes or until done.

Fresh Apple Cake

Hettie Jackson's recipe
Submitted by her daughter, Cynthia Brown

3 cups flour
2 cups sugar
1 tsp soda
1 tsp salt
½ tsp cinnamon
1 tsp nutmeg (optional)
2 eggs, beaten
1 cup salad oil
2 tsp vanilla
3 cups Winesap or Rome beauty apples, peeled and chopped (can use
     pears instead if desired)
1 cup chopped pecans

Combine and mix dry ingredients. Mix liquid ingredients separate. Add liquid ingredients to dry ingredients a little at a time. Batter will be very dry. Mix with a spoon. Add apples and nuts. Bake in greased, floured bundt pan at 350 degrees for one hour.

Icing:

1 stick margarine
1 large package cream cheese
1 box confectioner's sugar
1 tsp vanilla
1 cup nuts

Cream margarine and cream cheese together. Add sugar and vanilla. Mix well and stir in nuts.

"Everyone is kneaded out of the same dough but not baked in the same oven."

Yiddish Proverb

Chocolate Mayonnaise Cake

Submitted by Lisa Logan

2 cups flour
1 cup sugar
1 1/2 tsp baking soda
1 1/2 tsp baking powder
4 Tbsp. cocoa powder
1 cup cold water
1 cup mayonnaise
2 tsp vanilla

Mix dry ingredients together. Then add water and mix well. Add the mayonnaise and vanilla to the mixture and mix completely. Grease pans. Pour into 9x13 **or** 2 round cake pans. Bake at 350 degrees for 25 to 30 minutes or until a toothpick stuck in the middle comes out clean.

Chocolate Icing for Chocolate Mayonnaise Cake

2/3 cup butter, melted
2/3 cup cocoa
1 tsp vanilla
4 cups powdered sugar
4 Tbsp milk (more can be added if too thick)

Mix all ingredients together and mix well. It is enough to ice one 9x13 cake or two 8-to-9-inch round layers.

Cookies

Aunt Annies Cookies

Aunt Annies Cookies were famous amongst our church members and trickled out to the Bluff Dale Community. She soon gave up making other dishes for fellowships and funerals because her cookies were so sought after. Being her niece, I've watched and made cookies with her too many times to count.

The recipe is on the Toll House Semi-Sweet chocolate chip package. In her early years, she stirred and mixed it by hand, literally hands in the dough. When she got a Kitchen Aid, she let it do the stirring for her. The recipe is below, but bear in mind she could handle the dough in her hands like play dough, so more flour is needed to achieve Aunt Annie's texture. Enjoy!

Cynthia Brown

Chocolate Chip Cookies

Story and recipe submitted by Cynthia Brown

Cream together:
¾ cup white sugar
¾ cup brown sugar
1 cup white Crisco
Add:
2 eggs (while creaming)
1 tsp vanilla
Add:
2½ cups flour

*1 tsp soda (I add 1 tsp baking powder)

1 tsp salt

1½ - 2 cups chocolate chips (to taste)

1 cup pecans

I use a medium scoop to drop on sprayed with Pam cookie sheet.

Bake at 350 degrees 11-13 minutes.

Aunt Annie would take the dough out of the mixing bowl and add flour making dough stiff enough to handle. She would then pinch dough to place on cookie sheet. She also used silicone non-stick sheets on cookie sheet.

Soda makes them spread and baking powder makes them rise.

One More Anna's Cookies Story

For several years, the BDBC ladies gathered for sewing circle. Some ladies brought their knitting, embroidery, or sewing projects. Others brought different types of projects or none at all. We often went to Anna Watson's home, and there were always chocolate chip cookies. Anna noticed that Sherry Jacks ate the cookie part but picked out the chocolate chips. The next month, and every sewing circle thereafter, she baked several cookies with no chocolate chips just for Sherry. One of the many reasons we all loved Anna so much.

Wanda Strange

Nevaeh's Easy Tart Cherry Crisp

Nevaeh Hickman
Submitted by Melissa Saucedo

Mix Topping:
3/4 C brown sugar
1 C rolled oats
1/2 tsp cinnamon
6 TBSP butter, softened and cubed (cut it in)
1/2 C slivered almonds
   Mix and place in freezer.
Mix:
2 lbs. pitted cherries (2 frozen bags, thawed)
2 TBSP lemon juice
lemon zest (from 1 lemon)
1 tsp almond extract
Mix:
1/4 C cornstarch
3/4 C sugar
   Mix these two ingredients together then add to the cherry mixture above.
   Butter 6 - 8oz ramekins and fill w/ cherry mixture, then top with oat and almond topping/mixture. Bake @ 375 for 20-25 min. Top w/ vanilla bean ice cream or home-made whipped cream.

*"Commit to the Lord whatever you do, and he will establish your plans." (*Proverbs 16:3 NIV)

Chocolate Cookies

Submitted by Cynthia Brown

1 cup butter
2 cups sugar
2 eggs
3 tsp vanilla
3 cups flour
6 Tbsp cocoa
½ tsp salt
½ tsp baking powder
½ tsp soda

Cream first four ingredients. Add dry ingredients to creamed mixture. Add milk if needed. Add pecans if desired. Bake 350 degrees for 8 minutes.

Gluten-Free Peanut Butter Cookies

Submitted by Wanda Strange

2 Egg Whites
1 tsp vanilla
1 cup peanut butter (I use crunchy, but creamy works fine)

Beat egg whites with an electric mixer until it forms stiff peaks. Add vanilla and peanut butter and mix until well blended. Drop by spoonfuls onto lightly greased baking dish. Bake at 400 for 8-10 minutes or until lightly browned. Cool. (I sometimes spread the mixture into a sheet on the baking dish and cut into bars,)

Power Balls

Submitted by LaNell McNaughten

1 C peanut butter
1 C honey
1 t vanilla extract
3 C dry oatmeal
½ C Ground Flaxseed
½ C pecans
½ C dried craisins
½ C unsweetened coconut flakes
1 t cinnamon
1 T Chia seeds
1 C dark chocolate chips

In 2 C measuring cup measure 1 C honey. Add enough peanut butter to the cup to bring the mixture to 2 cups. Blend peanut butter and honey until smooth. Heating it may make it easier to combine. Add vanilla. Mix oats and flax seed in a large bowl. Add the rest of the dry ingredients to the bowl. Add the peanut butter and honey mixture to the dry ingredients. Stir until well combined. Add Chocolate chips (make sure the peanut butter has cooled enough that your chocolate doesn't melt). Cool and roll into small balls. Using wet hands or a wet cookie scoop makes this step easier. Store in airtight container in fridge or freezer.

Sugar Cookies

Submitted by Cynthia Brown

1 cup oleo (2 sticks)
1 cup confectioners' sugar

1 cup granulated sugar
2 eggs
1 cup oil
2 tsp vanilla
1 tsp soda
1 tsp cream of tartar

Cream oleo and confectioners' sugar, add white sugar. Beat in eggs until smooth. Add oil slowly. Stir in dry ingredients. Chill for easy handling. Shape into walnut size balls. Roll balls in granulated sugar. Place on greased baking sheet and press down with a glass. Bake at 375 degrees for 10 to 15 minutes.

Brownies

Submitted by Cynthia Brown

It is very important to make in correct order.
4 squares unsweetened chocolate
2 sticks margarine
2 cups sugar
1 tsp vanilla
1 cup pecans or walnuts
3 eggs, beaten
1 cup flour
Dash of salt

Melt chocolate and margarine in saucepan. Add sugar, vanilla, and nuts. Stir well and add eggs. Stir in flour and salt.

Bake at 350 degrees for 40 minutes in greased and floured Corning Ware pan.

Austin's Simply Delicious Chocolate Chip Cookies w/ Flash Freeze Option

Austin Saucedo
Submitted by Melissa Saucedo

3 C all-purpose flour
1 tsp baking soda
1/2 tsp baking powder
1 tsp salt
  Mix these ingredients. No need to sift. Set aside.
1 C salted butter (softened, not melted)
1 C granulated sugar
1 C brown sugar
  Cream these ingredients w/mixer.
Slowly add to the butter, sugar mixture:
2 Large Eggs
2 tsp Vanilla
  Beat until fluffy.
  Mix in dry ingredients you set aside (w/spatula not mixer). Do not overmix.
  If you would like to add any other mix-ins fold them in now, such as pecan or walnuts pieces, semi-sweet or milk chocolate chips.
  Scoop onto parchment paper (I love to use mini ice cream scoops).
  Bake@375 for no more than 9 min.
  To freeze for later or to give as a gift to a neighbor:
Flash freeze by scooping onto cookie sheet and placing in freezer for like 30 min. Then you can transfer to a giant baggie or freezer container. From frozen, bake @ 350 for no more than 15 min. Send frozen to a neighbor with a card of encouragement and these baking directions.

Other options: I have tried this recipe with other types of flour and sugar substitutes, they taste great. Look up swapping measurement ratios and have fun creating your own personalized recipe.

"Do not let any unwholesome talk come out of your mouths, but only what is helpful for building others up according to their needs, that it may benefit those who listen."
Ephesians 4:29 NIV

Praline Cookies

Submitted by Sherry Jacks

½ cup butter
½ cup brown sugar, packed
½ cup sugar
1 egg, lightly beaten
1½ cups all-purpose flour
1½ tsp. vanilla
1½ cups chopped pecans
Powdered sugar

Preheat oven to 375 degrees.

Microwave butter on high for 40-45 seconds or until butter is melted. Add sugars, egg, flour and vanilla. Mix well. Add pecans, mix well. Using small scoop, drop dough 2 inches apart onto cookie sheet. Bake 8-10 minutes until edges are slightly brown. Cool 2 minutes and remove to cooling rack. Sprinkle with powdered sugar.

"Sometimes Me think, 'What is a friend?' and then Me say, 'Friend is someone to share the last cookie with.'"
Cookie Monster

Pecan Pie Brownies

Submitted by Kerry Strange

Brownie Ingredients:
One brownie mix for 9x13 inch pan – prepare according to directions on the box
Pecan Pie Layer Ingredients:
1 cup granulated sugar
1 1/2 cups
4 eggs
1/4 cup butter
1 1/2 teaspoon
2 cups chopped
Instructions:
  Preheat oven according to brownie package instructions.
  Mix brownie batter according to package instructions.
  Combine the sugar, corn syrup, eggs, butter, and vanilla in a small saucepan and cook over medium heat stirring often.
  Pour brownie batter into a greased 13x9 inch baking dish and place in oven to bake for 15 minutes (half of the total bake time on your brownie package instructions).
  As the brownies bake the filling in the saucepan should have thickened enough to coat your spoon (about 15 minutes).
  Stir the chopped pecans into the mixture and continue to cook for 2-3 minutes more. (It should be a pourable consistency but not liquid.)
  When the brownies are done with their pre-baking, pour the pecan mixture over the top and gently spread it around to all of the edges.
  Place the baking dish back in the oven to bake an additional 25-30 minutes, or until the pecan pie layer is mostly set but still a little jiggly.
  Cool completely before serving.

Kahlua Brownies

From the kitchen of Bonnie Rucker
Story and recipe submitted to "Meals and Memories"

When I took Home Economics as a freshman in high school, the County Home Demonstration Agent visited our class. She gave us a lecture on cooking techniques and gave each of us a booklet of recipes. This brownie recipe was included. Through the years I've tried many others, but this one has remained my favorite. It must have been later in the 1970's that I added the Kahlua liqueur, having been gifted with a bottle and discovering the luxurious flavor it added to coffee or ice cream. Hence, my recipe for Kahlua Brownies.

2/3 cup butter
2/3 cup cocoa
2 cups sugar
4 eggs
1/3 oz Kahlua liqueur
2 tsp vanilla
1 1/3 cup flour
1 tsp baking powder
½ tsp salt
1 cup nuts (optional)

In a large mixing bowl, melt butter in microwave. By hand or on low mixer speed, stir in cocoa and sugar. Add eggs, one at a time. Add Kahlua liqueur and vanilla. Sift together flour, baking powder, and salt. Gradually stir in dry ingredients. Pour into a 9x12 inch pan sprayed with Pam or greased and floured. Bake at 350 degrees for 20-30 minutes or until done. These are best served warm without icing but can be iced with a favorite chocolate icing if desired.

Mrs. Lee's Orange Slice Cookies

Mrs. Lee's recipe submitted by Cynthia Brown

1 cup sugar
1 cup shortening
2 eggs
2 cups flour
1 tsp soda mixed with 4 Tbsp milk
2 cups oatmeal
1 small package of dates
1 cup nuts
1-2 cups candied orange slices
1 tsp vanilla
1 tsp salt
   Mix all ingredients. Drop by spoonful onto cookie sheet and bake at 350 degrees for 10-15 minutes.

Wedding Cookies

Submitted by Lisa Logan

1 lb (4 sticks) butter
4 cups flour
1 cup powdered sugar
1 tsp vanilla
1 cup pecans (optional)
   Mix all ingredients together. Divide dough into 3 equal parts and roll into rolls. Cover with plastic wrap or wax paper and freeze overnight. Remove from freezer and remove wrap and cut into cookies. Place on cookie sheet and bake on 350 degrees for 8 to 10

minutes. Bake until slightly brown on bottom. Remove from pan and cover with powdered sugar.

Boiled Cookies

Wanda Jaques (long time BDBC church member)
Submitted by Cynthia Brown

2 cups sugar
¼ cup cocoa
1 stick margarine
½ cup milk
Boil for 3 minutes
Add and stir:
1 tsp vanilla
½ cup peanut butter
Add:
2½ cup oats
   Drop onto wax paper

Cathey's Lemon Bars

Submitted by Cynthia Brown

1 cup flour
½ cup soft butter
¼ cup powdered sugar
   Mix and put in bottom of square pan.
   Press and bake for 15 minutes at 350 degrees.
   Beat 2 eggs till fluffy, add 3 Tbsp lemon juice, 1 cup sugar, 2 Tbsp flour. ½ tsp baking powder.
   Pour on crust bake 20-25 minutes at 350 degrees.
   Sprinkle with powdered sugar.

Biscotti

Submitted by Judy Bush

These are delicious with coffee. Enjoy!
Ingredients:
½ cup of butter
1 cup of sugar
2 Eggs
1 ½ tsp of vanilla
2 cups of flour
½ tsp of baking powder
½ tsp of baking soda
1 ½ cup of chopped nuts (we use almonds and pecans)
Cranberries or other dried fruits (optional, to taste)
Mix:
  Combine butter, sugar and eggs.
  Beat in vanilla
  Combine flour, baking powder, baking soda, nuts, and optional dried fruits
  Add to egg mixture.
  Cover and refrigerate for an hour or more
  Flour hands.
  Divide dough into two loaves about 12 inches long – should be like French bread.
  Grease cookie sheet and put loaves onto cookie sheet – about 3 inches apart.
  Flatten loaves slightly.
  Bake in preheated oven at 400 degrees for about 20 minutes.
  Remove and let cool slightly.
  Lower oven to 375 degrees.
  Slice warm loaves into diagonal strips about ½ inch thick.
  Return to oven and bake for about 15 minutes. Do not brown.

Neiman-Marcus Lemon Bars

Submitted by Sherry Jacks

Crust:
2 c. flour
1 c. butter
½ c. powdered sugar

Filling:
4 beaten eggs
½ c. lemon juice
½ tsp. baking powder
2 c. sugar
¼ c. flour
Grated lemon rind

Crust: Combine sugar, flour, and butter for crust. Use knife to cut in butter. Pat into 8x12x12 inch or 9x13 inch pan. Bake at 350 degrees for 20 minutes until lightly brown.

Filling: Combine eggs, sugar and lemon juice and beat. Add baking powder and flour. Beat until smooth. Pour into pan. Sprinkle lemon rind on top. Bake 25 minutes or until cake pulls away from sides. *Serves 15-20.*

Cobblers and Pies

Fruit Cobbler

Submitted by Wanda Strange

Ingredients:
1 stick butter or margarine
1 cup flour
1 cup sugar
1 Tbsp. baking powder
1 cup milk
Fruit – (fresh, frozen or canned) enough to cover the dish. I use 2 cans, partially drained. *Hint: If you are using fresh or frozen fruit, you may need to add granulated sugar to taste.*

Directions:
Place stick of butter in a 9x13 baking dish. Put dish in the oven while preheating to 350 degrees. While the butter is melting, mix dry ingredients. Add milk and stir well. When butter is melted, pour batter over the butter. DO NOT MIX. Drop fruit onto the batter. DO NOT MIX. Bake at 350 degrees for 45 minutes to an hour or until brown. The crust will rise to the top and be golden brown.

Blackberry Cobbler

Submitted by Renee Schott

This cobbler has been a big hit at Monday Evening Bible Study
¾ cup sugar
2 cups plus 1 tablespoon self-rising flour (see note)
2 cups fresh blackberries
¼ cup (1/2 stick) butter, cold, cut into small pieces
½ to 2/3 cup milk
Vanilla ice cream for serving

Preheat the oven to 450 degrees. Butter a 1-quart casserole dish or baking pan.

In a medium saucepan combine the sugar, 1 tablespoon of the flour, berries, and 1 cup water. Bring to a boil, reduce the heat, and simmer for 2 minutes, then remove from the heat and set aside.

In a medium bowl, use a pastry blender or two knives to cut the butter into the remaining 2 cups flour. Stir in just enough milk to make a soft dough that pulls away from the sides of the bowl. Turn the dough out on a lightly floured board and pat into a square. Use a rolling pin to roll it to ½ inch thick. Cut the dough into 2-inch strips.

Pour 1 cup of the blackberry mixture into the bottom of the pan. Arrange half of the dough strips on top of the blackberry mix, placing them close together. Bake until brown, about 12 minutes. Then remove from the oven and pour the remaining berry mixture over the baked strips. Arrange another layer of dough strips on top and bake for 12 more minutes, or until brown. Serve warm with ice cream.

"Fruit trees of all kinds will grow on both banks of the river. Their leaves will not wither, nor will their fruit fail. Every month they will bear fruit, because the water from the sanctuary flows to them. Their fruit will serve for food and their leaves for healing." (Ezekiel 47:12 NIV)

Oil Pastry

Submitted by Cynthia Brown

1½ cups flour
½ tsp salt
¼ cup milk
½ cup Crisco oil

Combine flour and salt. Make a well and add milk and oil to the well. With fork toss flour into well. Scrape sides. Loosely make ball and pour into pie pan. Using fingers, press dough in pan. Prick with fork. Bake at 350 for 25 minutes or until brown. Can also be used unbaked for fruit pies.

Peanut Butter Pie

Submitted by Bliss Woodyard
First place award winning recipe

9-inch prepared graham cracker crust
1 8-ounce package cream cheese
½ cup peanut butter (spray measuring cup with Pam for easy release)
½ cup confectioners' sugar
1 16-ounce container of whipped topping thawed

Mix cream cheese, peanut butter, confectioner's sugar and ½ of whipped topping.

Spoon into the crust. Place remaining whipped topping over peanut butter mixture. Enjoy!

Two Blueberry Pies

Submitted by Cynthia Brown

2 graham cracker crusts
4 medium bananas
1 cup sugar
8 ounces cream cheese
1 envelope Dream Whip or 12 oz Cool Whip
1 can Lucky Leaf blueberry pie filling

Cut up bananas on the bottom of the crust. Mix sugar and cream cheese. Prepare Dream Whip as directed. Then mix w/ cheese mixture and put on top of bananas. Top w/ pie filling. Chill.

Makes two pies.

Easy Key Lime Pie

Here's our family's favorite easy dessert

Submitted by Andrea Blount

Ingredients:
1 9-inch graham cracker crust
8 ounces cream cheese, softened
1 14-ounce can sweetened condensed milk
1/2 cup Key Lime Juice
1 teaspoon vanilla
Directions:
Cream the cheese with an electric mixer. Add the condensed milk and the vanilla to the cream cheese mixture, beating until well blended. Add the lime juice and beat it into the mixture thoroughly. Pour the mixture into the crust and cool thoroughly in the refrigerator. Top with either Cool whip or whipped cream and refrigerate again.

Mrs. Kittles Pecan Pie

Submitted by Cynthia Brown

3 eggs
1 cup syrup (White Karo)
1 cup pecans (cut in small pieces)
½ cup sugar
1 tsp vanilla
½ salt
Cinnamon/sugar mixture, to taste

Beat eggs slightly (do not use an electric mixer). Add sugar, syrup, nuts, salt and vanilla. Mix well, put in unbaked pie shell and lightly sprinkle cinnamon sugar on top. Bake 50 minutes in slow oven at 300.

Crustless Buttermilk Pie

Submitted by Cynthia Brown

1 1/3 cup sugar
1 cup buttermilk
2 cups Bisquick
1/3 cup butter melted
1 tsp vanilla
3 large eggs
Dash of salt

Blend until smooth. Bake in sprayed 9-inch pan at 350 degrees for 40-50 minutes or until done.

Chocolate Ice Box Pie

**Elaine Block's Award-Winning Recipe
Submitted by her sister, Cynthia Brown**

*One year, Cheryl Barron, organized church members to
host a Community October Fest. One of the activities was
a pie contest. Elaine's wonderful Chocolate Ice Box Pie took
first prize. Here's the recipe.*

3 egg yolks
½ cup milk
1 large can carnation milk
Sift:
1 cup sugar
3 Tbsp cocoa
3 Tbsp flour (leveled)
Pinch salt
   Combine first three ingredients. Blend in dry ingredients. Cook
for 8 minutes until bubbles pop.
   Add 1 Tbsp vanilla. Pour into prepared/baked crust. Refrigerate.

After I graduated from TCU in my early twenties, I was hired to teach Home Economics at my former High School, Eastern Hills in Fort Worth. In those days learning to be a home maker was still an honorable profession. Half the year I taught girls how to cook and the other half year how to sew. Demonstration was the teaching style I used. I gave the girls the recipes I demonstrated to make with their group in the cooking lab. I shared the Meringue Pie recipe which I acquired from my former high school Home Ec teacher, Marguarite Thompson. She taught me both my junior and senior years at Eastern Hills. Then four years later I returned to teach with her.

Cynthia Brown

Easy Microwave Cream Pie

This is the recipe I gave my home ec class.

Submitted by Cynthia Brown

1/3 cup flour
2/3 cup sugar
½ tsp salt
2 cups milk
2 Tbsp margarine
3 slightly beaten egg yolks

Mix flour, salt, and sugar. Add milk, margarine, and egg yolks. Cook in microwave for 8 minutes, stirring every 2 minutes. (Can cook on stovetop for 8 minutes.) Add vanilla.

Variations:

Coconut: Add 1 cup coconut.
Butterscotch: Substitute 1 cup brown sugar for granulated sugar.

Chocolate: use ¼ cup flour, 4 TBSP cocoa, and 1 cup sugar.

Lemon Cream: Use 1 cup sugar and juice of 2 lemons or Realemon.

Pineapple: Add 1 cup pineapple, 1/3 cup plus 1 TBSP flour, and ½ tsp vanilla.

Best Buttermilk Pie

Submitted by Cynthia Brown

Take your choice between vanilla and lemon-flavored buttermilk pie. Better still, try it both ways.

1 unbaked 9-inch pie shell
½ cup butter
1 cup sugar
3 eggs
3 Tbsp flour
1 cup buttermilk
Dash nutmeg
1 tsp vanilla or ½ tsp lemon flavoring

Cream butter and sugar well. Add eggs one at a time. Beat until fluffy. Add flour and blend well. Fold in buttermilk and nutmeg. Add vanilla or lemon flavoring. Pour into pie shell. Bake at 350 degrees for one hour or until knife inserted in the center comes out clean.

Give everyone a chance to have a piece of the pie. If the pie's not big enough, make a bigger pie.
                                        Dave Thomas

Chocolate Pie

From the kitchen of Anna Watson
As submitted to "Meals and Memories"

I love to make pies. My daughter, Carolyn, was just a baby, when she discovered a chocolate pie on the table and proceeded to pull it down to the floor and help herself. Below is my chocolate pie recipe, which I find easy and no fail.

2 cups milk
3 eggs
1 cup sugar
3 Tbsp flour
3 Tbsp cocoa
2 Tbsp butter or margarine
1 Tbsp vanilla

Pour milk into a medium saucepan and put on the stove to heat. Using two bowls, separate eggs, whites in one bowl and yolks in the other. Add sugar, flour, cocoa, and about ½ cup of the warm milk to the yolks. Beat well and add back into the hot milk in the saucepan. Continue to cook until thickened. Remove from the stove top and add butter and vanilla. Mix well. Pour into cooked pie crust. Put meringue on top and finish baking until meringue is lightly brown. Cool pie before cutting.

3 egg whites
3 Tbsp Sugar
½ tsp cream of tartar

Beat egg whites with your Kitchen Aide Mixer until stiff and they stand in peaks. Add sugar and cream of tartar. Pile on top of pie filling and bake in 350-degree oven until brown.

Never Fail Meringue

Allene McCormick
Submitted by her daughter, Cheryl McCormick Roades

1 tbsp cornstarch
½ cup water
Few grains of salt
6 Tbsp sugar
3 egg whites

Mix cornstarch, sugar, water and salt in saucepan, cook until thick and clear. Cool slightly. Beat egg whites with electric mixer until foamy; continue beating while pouring to cornstarch mixture. Beat 5 minutes.

With two older sisters, all of us coming from a long line of fantastic cooks, I remember best the recipe for pie crust Wanda Strange included in my other sister's recipe box gift. It said simply, "Go to the store and buy one." She later added, "Be sure to remove the paper lining from between the crusts." For the first Thanksgiving of her married life, Wanda proudly baked a pecan pie for Kerry's family. Despite the beautiful presentation, when they cut into it, they discovered the lining between the filling and crust. To her mother-in-law's credit, she didn't make it a big deal out of the mistake, but it definitely became a joke for all of our family.

Lisa Bell

Coconut Cream Pie

Allene McCormick
Submitted by her daughter, Cheryl McCormick Roades

½ cup sugar
1/8 tsp salt
1 ½ cups scalded milk
1 tsp vanilla
1 Tbsp butter
5 Tbsp flour
¼ cups cold milk
3 egg yolks
1 cup shredded coconut

Blend sugar, flour and salt with the cold milk; add scalded milk, stirring constantly. Cook slowly until thick. Add beaten yolks; cook 2 minutes longer. Remove from range; add vanilla, coconut and butter. Cool; pour into a baked pie shell. Cover top with meringue; bake at 350 degrees until meringue is brown (about 15 minutes) Yield: 6 large servings.

I add additional coconut to the top of the meringue before browning.

Pumpkin Custard Pie

From the Kitchen of Nelda Estes
As submitted to "Meals and Memories"

3 unbaked pie shells
1 large can Libby pumpkin (or 1½ small cans)
3 cups sugar

½ cup flour
9 eggs, separated (set whites aside)
1 tsp cinnamon
1 tsp salt
½ tsp nutmeg
3 cups whole milk

Mix all ingredients and then blend in milk. Beat egg whites until stiff, then fold into the mixture. Pour into unbaked pie shells and bake at 350 degrees approximately 1½ hours until firm to touch and top is brown. Keep a close watch while baking so not to burn.

Ice Cream

Ice Cream Sermon

Small town traditions are a huge part of what holds our Bluff Dale Community together. As Don and I were attempting to make the life changing move from Fort Worth to Bluff Dale, to build a new home on family land deeded to us from my mother, we attended the annual ice cream social hosted by the Garden Club.

When we walked into the gathering, all eyes turned toward the new couple. As if on cue, adding to our grand entrance, I stumbled and fell down. Don turned to me, and as is so him, said, "I can't take you anywhere."

Thus, we entered our life in a small town.

Years later it became my job, as a member and officer of Bluff Dale Garden and Study Club, to organize the Community July Ice Cream Social. One particular year, I grabbed the ice cream freezer, stored in the car port, preparing to make my home-made ice cream. But alas, the freezer would not chug to life. Not to be deterred from my homemade ice cream making duty, I went to Braums and purchased Mint Chocolate Chip Ice Cream. In an attempt to keep it frozen in the July Heat, I emptied the Braums cartons into the silver cylinder of the ice cream freezer and shoved the cylinder into my freezer to stay cold.

When the time came, I took the cylinder from the freezer packed it in ice in the wooden bucket and carried it to the social. As a part of the tradition, each lady stands behind her freezer to serve her own ice cream. I served Braum's ice cream, disguised as homemade. To my total surprise, guests offered unexpected compliments.

"This ice cream is so good."

"Do you share your recipe?"

"Can I have seconds, please?"

To which I just smiled and said, "Thank you."

Now, the next day was Sunday. My Children's sermon focused on the subject of lying.

Cynthia Brown

My Introduction to the Ice Cream Social and BDBC Children's Sermon

The Community Ice Cream Social introduced me to the traditions of Bluff Dale. Gathering and getting to know new friends highlighted the evening. The temptation of homemade ice cream and baked goodies made for a "must do" event. The welcoming atmosphere and the apparent community bonds confirmed, "This is the place I can feel at home."

I connected quickly and looked forward to the time I could retire and participate fully in the events of the community and the church.

Bluff Dale Baptist differed from the large inner city Dallas church we attended. The warmth of the people welcomed us, and one thing that seemed familiar was the children's sermon.

I loved Cynthia's children's sermons. She spoke plainly to the children in a way they could understand and with a point that challenged the adults.

I honestly don't remember the mint chocolate chip ice cream, but I vividly recall her confession to the children. She gave some examples of lying. Then she told the children what she had done. She asked them, "Is letting my friends think I made the ice cream lying?"

The sweet little children didn't quite know how to

respond to their kindergarten teacher.

Cynthia prompted them. "Yes, what I did was wrong. Making them think it was homemade deceived them and that is the same as lying."

I may forget specific flavors and foods, but I'll always remember the friends and the fun times we share. I don't always remember specific sermons, but this simple message stuck with me for more than two decades.

Wanda Strange

Homemade Vanilla Ice Cream

Submitted by Wanda Strange

6 Egg Whites (beaten until stiff peaks form)
6 Egg Yolks (beaten)
Fold egg yolks into stiffly beaten egg whites
Add 1 Can sweetened condensed milk (Eagle Brand or similar)
1 Tbsp Vanilla (or more for desired taste)
More sugar can be added for additional sweetness if desired.
   Pour mixture into ice cream freezer canister.
   Add milk to fill cannister to the fill line.
   Freeze in ice cream freezer
   Variations:
   Add fruit or crushed candies or cookies for different flavors

"Life is like an ice cream cone, you have to lick it one day at a time."

Charles M. Schultz

Easy Soda Ice Cream

Submitted by Wanda Strange and Lisa Bell

1 2-liter bottle soda (Orange Crush, Big Red, or another fruity flavor)
1 can Eagle Brand sweetened condensed milk
Milk to fill canister

Pour all ingredients into ice-cream freezer canister.

Freeze per ice cream maker instructions.

Peanut Butter Ice Cream

Submitted by Wanda Strange and Lisa Bell

Our dad made the best peanut butter ice cream. As the youngest, Lisa often sat on the hand-cranked ice cream maker and got the first taste.

3/4 cup smooth peanut butter
2/3 cup sugar (less if desired)
3 cups half-n-half
1 tsp vanilla
1/8 tsp salt
Add milk to fill canister if necessary
Optional add-ins: Oreo cookies (chopped and frozen), peanut cups (chopped and frozen), Reese's Pieces candy.

Beat peanut butter and sugar until smooth.

Slowly beat in 1 cup half-n-half until thoroughly combined.

Whisk in 2 cups half-n-half, vanilla, and salt.

Freeze according to manufacturer's instructions. Add mix-ins during last five minutes.

Homemade Ice Cream (Custard Cooked)

Hettie Harris Jackson – Effie Harris – Cynthia Brown
Family recipe passed down

5 eggs separated, add whites beaten stiff, last
2½ cups of sugar (or less)
1 heaping Tbsp flour
2 cups milk
1 can canned milk

Cook until bubbles pop and custard thickens. Add 1 teaspoon vanilla. Pour into 1-gallon freezer. Finish filling with milk or 1 quart whipping cream(optional) Freeze.

> *"Hear, Israel, and be careful to obey so that it may go well with you and that you may increase greatly in a land flowing with milk and honey, just as the Lord, the God of your ancestors, promised you." (Deuteronomy 6:3 NIV).*

Why is it some women are complimented when asked to share a recipe and some guard their recipes as if sacred to their abilities as cooks. Such a woman graced our town and her cooking skills were impeccable. However, what was hers to know, was only yours to imagine.
Each year she brought her famous "Apricot" ice cream to the community ice cream social. It was just as good as I had heard. Being the newbie in town and unaware of such guarded secrets, I asked said lady for her recipe, to which she replied, "Yes" and proceeded to speak her guarded Apricot Ice Cream recipe to me.

The secret's out and yours to enjoy, because recipes un-shared die with the guardian, but if shared, live on to grace and bless others.

Cynthia Brown

Apricot Ice Cream

Submitted by Cynthia Brown

Add to Homemade Ice Cream (Custard Cooked) recipe above.
2 small packages apricot Jello (should match fruit)
2 cans apricots, chopped (substitute peaches, strawberries, or other fruit as desired)
Add the juice from the apricots to other liquids.
1 quart whipping cream
   Pour into ice cream freezer. Finish filling with milk if needed. Freeze.

Bluff Dale Community Ice Cream Social July 2023

All the time I lived away from Bluff Dale, my mother, Effie Harris, would invite us to the Garden Club Ice Cream Social. It has been going on for many years and is looked forward to by the whole town. Just think about 15 or more freezers of homemade ice cream sitting side by side, all of them just waiting to be eaten! The good news is that you can keep going back as long as there is any ice cream in the freezers. Here is my mother's recipe (she always made vanilla). But people love Butterfinger ice cream, so I added my alterations to her recipe to make Butterfinger

Anna Watson

Homemade Vanilla (or Butterfinger) Ice Cream

From the kitchen of Anna Watson
Story and recipe submitted to "Meals and Memories"

2 cups milk
5 eggs separated
2 Tbsp flour
3 cups sugar
1 Tbsp vanilla
1 quart whipping cream
1 large can Carnation evaporated milk
Whole milk
5 or 6 crushed Butterfinger candy bars

Put 2 cups of milk on stovetop to steam.

Beat egg whites until they peak. Add yolks, sugar and flour and mix well.

Put in hot milk and cook until it thickens.

Add vanilla and candy bars, then pour mixture into canister. Add whipping cream, evaporated milk, and enough whole milk to finish filling the canister to the freeze line.

Freeze as you would any homemade ice cream.

Dressings,
Sauces,
Bar-b-que
Sauce, Salsas

Homemade Picante Sauce

Mary Anne Foreman
Story and Recipe submitted by Renee Gresham

Mary Anne was famous for this recipe. She grew lots of tomatoes and peppers every summer so that she could make this. I never made it myself but I was sure glad to eat it.

1-gallon fresh tomatoes
8-10 jalapenos, sliced
2 large onions, chopped
½ cup vinegar
¼ cup salt
1 small bottle hot and spicy ketchup

Skin tomatoes and cut into chunks. Mix everything together in a large kettle. Simmer over low heat until mixture thickens, about 30-40 minutes. Pour into clean Mason jars and process in a boiling, hot water bath for 15 minutes.

Processing recommended by Extension Service.

Boiled Dressing

Effie Harris
Submitted by her granddaughter, Cynthia Brown

1 egg
2 Tbsp vinegar
1 cup sugar
2/3 cup milk
Pinch salt

Combine and cook to boil. Can be stored in refrigerator.
(Good for Apple Salad)

Robinett Blender Salsa

Submitted by Terri Robinett

16-oz can stewed tomatoes
3-4 medium sized canned jalapenos, stems removed (I usually just use
    from a jar...too easy!)
1 tsp garlic salt
1 Tbsp vinegar (can use apple cider vinegar)
1 tsp sugar
3 Tbsp chopped green onions
    Combine all ingredients in a blender and blend for about 30 sec-
onds. You could add Cilantro if you like, but Edd doesn't like, so I
don't.

Pepper Relish

From the kitchen of Anna Watson
As submitted to "Meals and Memories"

This relish recipe came from my aunt, Opal Harris Pittman.
1 pint ground sweet peppers
1 pint ground green tomatoes
1 pint ground onions
1 pint sugar
1 pint vinegar
1-pint prepared mustard
1 hot pepper to taste
    Mix all ingredients and cook slowly about one hour or until thick.
Put into clean jars and process in boiling water bath for 15 minutes.

Refrigerator Pickles

Submitted by Becky Rodrique

6 cups thinly sliced cucumbers
2 cups thinly sliced onions
1½ cups sugar
1½ cups white vinegar
½ tsp pickling salt (uniodized salt)
½ tsp mustard seeds
½ tsp celery seeds
½ tsp turmeric

In several glass canning jars, alternately layer the cucumbers and onions. In a medium-size saucepan, combine the sugar, vinegar, salt and spices. Bring to a boil and stir until the sugar dissolves. Pour the syrup over the veggies. Cool. Cover tightly and refrigerate for at least 24 hours before using. These pickles will keep for several months in the fridge.

Sometimes there are more veggies than syrup, so be prepared to make another batch of syrup if necessary – or cut up fewer veggies.

Several years after Aunt Annie's first husband, Hershell, died (around 1986), Aunt Annie joined her daughter Carolyn, son-in-law, Jay, and one of Jay's friends to participate in competitive barbeque cook-offs. They needed a name for their group. Don gave the suggestion of "Barbie and Ques." The name stuck. Below is Jay's B-B-Q Sauce recipe used on their prize-winning barbeque.

Aunt Annie was the Barbie in the group. The two men were the ques.

Cynthia Brown

Jay B-B-Q Sauce

**Jay Stemple award winning recipe
Submitted by his cousin-in-law, Cynthia Brown**

4 Tbsp bacon drippings
2 cups catsup
½ cup molasses
¼ cup vinegar
2 Tbsp Worcestershire Sauce
   Heat together.
Add:
2 Tbsp chili powder
½ tsp salt
½ tsp cayenne pepper
½ tsp garlic powder
1½ cup water
   Boil 10 minutes.
   Reduce heat and simmer for 45 minutes
   Let cool 1-2 hours.
   Makes 1 quart.

Breads

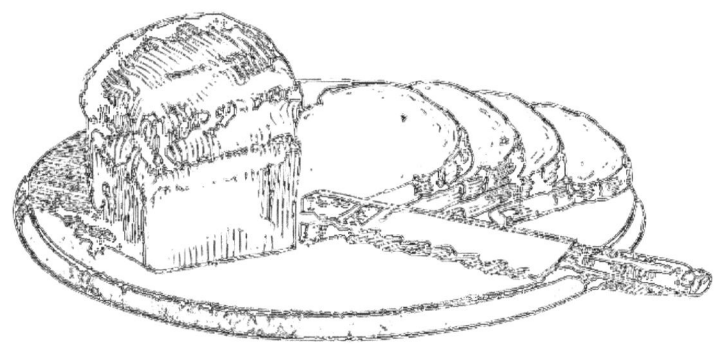

Perfect Sweet Cornbread

Submitted by Lisa Logan

1 cup flour
¼ cup sugar
1 cup yellow cornmeal
4 tsp baking powder
¾ tsp salt
2 eggs
1 cup milk
¼ cup oil
Mix dry ingredients together and stir in eggs, milk and oil. Pour into greased pan. Bake at 350 degrees for 20 to 25 minutes.

Buttery Biscuit Rolls

Jean Tucker's recipe
Submitted by her cousin, Cynthia Brown

2 sticks (1/2 lb butter) Do Not substitute margarine.
1 8-ounce container sour cream
2 cups self-rising flour
   Preheat oven to 350 degrees.
   Melt butter in saucepan and remove from heat.
   Add sour cream and flour. Mix well.
   Drop batter into greased mini-muffin tins, filling to the top.
   Bake 25 minutes.
   Makes 2 dozen rolls.

Janet's Bread

Janet Crum's recipe
Submitted by Cynthia Brown

1½ packages yeast
2 cups warm water
1 Tbsp salt
1/3 cup shortening
1/3 cup sugar
Flour to desired consistency

 Dissolve yeast in warm water. Stir in salt, shortening, and sugar.
 Add flour until dough is the consistency of play dough.
 Let rise in fridge overnight.
 Knead and pinch into rolls or form into loaf.
 Let rise 30 minutes to an hour. Bake at 350 for 15 minutes.

Variation:

 For Cinnamon rolls:2

 Roll out to approximately 16"x20"

 Melt 1/3 cup butter. Pour and spread over dough. Mix together 1 cup brown sugar, 2 Tbsp cinnamon, 1. Spread mixture over rolled out dough.

 Roll dough into a log and cut into 1- to 1 1/4-inch slices to form cinnamon rolls.

 Let rise. Bake at 350 for 15 minutes.

Icing:

8 Tbsp butter
1½ cup powdered sugar
¼ cup cream cheese
½ tsp vanilla
½ tsp salt

 Pour over cinnamon rolls.

"Food is art, and you are the artist."

Unknown

Garlic Cheddar Beer Bread

Submitted by Beverly Holmes

Whip up a loaf of this Garlic Cheddar Beer Bread in practically no time and with no yeast. Can easily be doubled to make 2 loaves. Bread is great with butter, toasted or with a bowl of chili or soup. This bread is always a big hit at Monday night Ladies Bible Study.

   Prep time: 10 minutes
   Cook Time: 45 minutes
   Total time: 55 minutes

Ingredients

3 cups all-purpose flour
2½ Tbsp granulated sugar
1 Tbsp baking powder
1 tsp kosher salt
1-2 tsp garlic powder (depending on how garlicky you want it)
1 cup shredded cheddar cheese
12 ounces beer
3 Tbsp melted butter

Garlic Butter topping

2 ½ tbsp melted butter
1 tsp dried parsley (or 1 Tbsp minced fresh parsley)
½ tsp garlic powder

Instructions

   1. Preheat oven to 350 degrees F and lightly spray the sides of 9x5" loaf pan. Set aside

2. In a mixing bowl, add flour, sugar, baking powder salt, garlic powder and stir to combine. Stir in the shredded cheese. Make a little well in the center of the dry ingredients.

3. Pour in the beer and stir until no remaining flour streaks remain

4. Add half the melted butter to the bottom of the prepared loaf pan and tilt the pan around so the butter coats the bottom of the pan. Transfer the batter to the pan, spreading out into an even layer.

5. Pour the remaining half of the melted butter over the top of the batter, brushing it around so it evenly coats the top.

6. Bake for 45-50 minutes, until golden brown and a toothpick inserted in the center comes out clean or with just a few moist crumbs.

7. Whisk together garlic butter topping ingredients. (melted butter, parsley, garlic powder) and brush over the top of the loaf once it comes out of the oven.

8. Let bread cool in the pan for 5-7 minutes, brush again with any left-over garlic butter topping. Turn out carefully onto a wire rack to finish cooling.

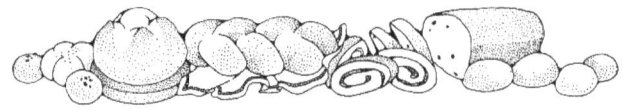

Jesus answered, "It is written: 'Man shall not live
by bread alone, but on every word that comes from
the mouth of God.'" (Matthew 4:4 NIV).

Cornbread

Submitted by Judy Warden

1 box Jiffy cornbread (corn muffin) mix. Jiffy is sweet ... you want a
    sweet mix.
2 eggs, slightly beaten
1 SMALL (8.25 oz.) can cream corn
½ cup oil (I use canola.)
1 small can chopped green chilies, undrained (I use "mild.")
    Preheat oven to 350 degrees.
    Combine all and bake, uncovered, in an 8x8 or 9x9 greased dish,
45-50 minutes until cracking and golden. Easy to double and bake
in a 9x13 pan – just bake a little longer.
    Everyone loves this. It does tend to fall apart, as it is very moist,
but no one cares. No butter needed. You could eat with a fork, but
fingers work just as well !

Yeast Rolls

Story and recipe submitted by Cynthia Brown

My grandmother, Effie Roades Harris, was born, raised and died in Bluff Dale. She was a lifetime member of Bluff Dale Baptist Church. I remember coming to Bluff Dale on Sundays to visit and go to church with her and my Granddaddy, Alvin Harris. The yeast roll recipe came from her mother, Lula Elua Rhoades.

1 cup milk	2 cups milk	3 cups milk
1 heaping Tbsp sugar	2 heaping Tbsp sugar	3 heaping Tbsp sugar
1 tsp salt	2 tsp salt	3 tsp salt
1 heaping Tbsp Crisco	2 heaping Tbsp Crisco	3 heaping Tbsp Crisco
1 package yeast	2 packages yeast	3 packages yeast

Choose the appropriate column for single, double, or triple recipe.

Combine above ingredients. Add flour until the dough is the consistency of play dough. Knead and pinch into rolls. Let rise and bake.

Helpful Hints

Helpful Hints from Karen

Karen Strange Cunningham

My sister-in-law, an incredible cook, offered some practical hints in a family cookbook compiled many years ago. I share them with you in memory of Karen. Wanda Strange

- After grating cheese, run a hard crust of bread over the grater to clean it.

- Fresh Celery leaves dropped in the pot while cooking shrimp helps destroy the odor.

- Rub salt generously over a cracked egg and you can successfully boil it.

- For ease in getting a thinly rolled pie crust off the board and into the pie pan, fold lightly in half, then in half again. Unfold in the pie pan.

- If you only need half an onion at a time, save the root half. It will last longer.

- Chopped fruit and nuts will be more evenly dispersed in cake batter if they are lightly floured before added.

- A little butter rubbed on the underside of the cream pitcher spout will keep cream from dripping after it is poured.

- Always break lettuce in bite size pieces. Never cut it with a knife.

- Add sugar to fresh green vegetables before cooking. This improves the flavor.

- Add hot water to vegetables when cooking to keep the vegetables from being tough.

- Keep berries refrigerated, uncovered until just before using, then wash gently. Drain well in a sieve or colander.

- Add diced bits of avocado as topping for hot consommé for special eye appeal.

- To keep potato slices from discoloring, soak them in water to which lemon juice has been added.

Safe Substitutions

Submitted by Wanda Strange

These are the substitutions my sister-in-law shared with me when we were both newly married.

INSTEAD OF...	USE
1 cup of fresh milk	½ cup evaporated milk plus ½ cup water (or) ¼ cup dried skim milk powder plus 1 cup water and 1 tsp melted fat or salad oil.
1 cup sour milk (buttermilk)	1 cup fresh, sweet milk plus 1-1/3 Tbsp lemon juice
1 square (1 oz) sweetened chocolate	2 Tbsp Cocoa plus 1 Tbsp shortening
1 tsp baking powder	¼ tsp soda and ½ tsp. cream of tartar

"Food is not just eating energy. It's an experience."
Guy Fieri

Dawn Spray for dishes

Submitted by Cynthia Brown

Dawn Ultra Platinum Powerwash dish spray
 Makes 16 ounces
 Combine and place in spray bottle
 13 oz water
 2 oz (1/4 cup) blue Dawn
 1 oz (2 Tbsp) alcohol

Upsize Cake

Submitted by Cynthia Brown

Cake mixes use to be 18 oz. Now they are 15.6.
 To upsize cake, I keep these mixed ingredients in an airtight container and add 1/3 cup to make the skimpy 15.6 oz into an 18 oz mix.
 1½ cup flour
 1 cup sugar
 2 tsp baking powder
 ¼ tsp soda
 Mix together and store in fridge.

And those who can't cook get left with doing the dishes.

References

Bramen, L. (2010, May 25). *Good Night and Good Potluck.* Retrieved July 4, 2024, from Smithsonian Magazine: https://www.smithsonianmag.com/arts-culture/good-night-and-good-potluck-89186862/#:~:text=According%20to%20Foodtimeline.org%2C%20the,print%20in%20the%2015th%20century.

Lemm, Elaine. 2019. "Top Tips for Working With Chocolate." The Spruce Eats. December 3. Accessed July 6, 2024. https://www.thespruceeats.com/tips-for-working-with-chocolate-435491#What%20Is%20Chocolate?

Watson, Anna Belle Harris. 2006. Bluff Dale: People and Places in the Heart. The Booklet Place, Inc.

About Bluff Dale Baptist Church

Located in the small community of Bluff Dale, Texas, the church began in July 1874 as Friendship Baptist Church, under the direction of brothers, J.C.R. Lockhart and B.F Lockhart. B.C. Harris served as the first pastor. Descendents of many charter members remain active in the church today. On April 5, 1876, the name changed to Bluff Springs. Later, on the Saturday before the first Sunday in June 1878, the name became Bluff Dale Baptist Church.

In the early years, the schoolhouse hosted the congregation in winter. As weather warmed, they moved to the brush arbor. In 1893, the church raised funds for a building to be located on land given by A.J. Glenn.

While the church struggled through heresy, splits, the Great Depression, and many trials, it remains a beacon for the community with faithful members who seek God's Word and direction. Although imperfect, the congregation strives to follow the covenant created long ago.[1]

"Now the God of peace, who brought again from the dead our Lord Jesus that great Shepherd of the sheep, through the blood of the everlasting Covenant, make you perfect in every good work to do his will, working in you, that which is well pleasing in His sight, through Jesus Christ: To whom be glory forever and ever. Amen."

425 Glenn St., Bluff Dale, TX.
(254) 728-3712
For more information about Bluff Dale Baptist Church visit
https://www.facebook.com/BluffDaleBaptistChurch/

---

1. Watson 2006

With Gratitude...

To those who shared recipes and stories, thank you for your time and effort. We would not have this cookbook without you.

Cynthia Brown, Sherry Jacks, Terri Robinett, and Judy Warden—you ladies perfected the text with grammatical skills, attention to details, and your valued cooking expertise.

Lisa Bell, thank you for your expertise and generous use of your knowledge and talents. We greatly appreciate the hours of work you donated to complete this project.

May God bless you all for contributing to this cookbook and continually providing the time-tested recipes at many community events. While this book came from Bluff Dale Baptist Church, the entire community of this small town comes together, supporting values which make Bluff Dale an amazing place to live.

www.ingramcontent.com/pod-product-compliance
Lightning Source LLC
Chambersburg PA
CBHW051311120626
46547CB00015B/2184